CRIMINAL JUSTICE IN ISRAEL

Recent Titles in
Research and Bibliographical Guides in Criminal Justice

Criminal Activity in the Deep South, 1700–1930: An Annotated Bibliography
A. J. Wright, compiler

Criminal Justice Ethics: Research and Bibliographical Guide
Frank Schmalleger, compiler, with the assistance of Robert McKenrick

Comparative Criminology: An Annotated Bibliography
Piers Beirne and Joan Hill, compilers

CRIMINAL JUSTICE IN ISRAEL

An Annotated Bibliography of English Language Publications, 1948–1993

Compiled by *Robert R. Friedmann*

Research and Bibliographical Guides in Criminal Justice, Number 4

GREENWOOD PRESS
Westport, Connecticut • London

Library of Congress Cataloging-in-Publication Data

Friedmann, Robert R.
Criminal justice in Israel : an annotated bibliography of English language publications, 1948–1993 / compiled by Robert R. Friedmann.
p. cm.—(Research and bibliographical guides in criminal justice, ISSN 1042–4636 ; no. 4)
Includes bibliographical references and index.
ISBN 0–313–29439–9 (alk. paper)
1. Crime—Israel—Bibliography. 2. Criminal justice, Administration of—Israel—Bibliography. 3. Criminal law—Israel—Bibliography. I. Title. II. Series.
Z5703.5.I75F75 1995
[HV7078.5]
016.36495694—dc20 94–39770

British Library Cataloguing in Publication Data is available.

Library of Congress Catalog Card Number: 94–39770
ISBN: 0–313–29439–9
ISSN: 1042–4636

First published in 1995

Greenwood Press, 88 Post Road West, Westport, CT 06881
An imprint of Greenwood Publishing Group, Inc.

Printed in the United States of America

The paper used in this book complies with the Permanent Paper Standard issued by the National Information Standards Organization (Z39.48–1984).

10 9 8 7 6 5 4 3 2 1

Contents

Preface

In the Summer of 1992 Georgia State University offered, for the first time ever (for this or any other U.S. university), a studies abroad program on criminal justice that took students to Israel. As part of the preparation for the course, I made an effort to assemble for the students a bibliography in English. During the search for bibliographical sources I had realized that the extent of English-based references is far greater than originally expected.

In the Summer of 1991, the Henrietta Szold Institute published a source book of Hebrew language references, edited by Menachem Amir and Dina Shur. The source book contained Hebrew reference material published between 1948 and 1991 on crime, juvenile delinquency and corrections in Israel. I mentioned to Menachem Amir my intentions to publish collected references in English and thus offer the interested reader a complete reference service in both languages, and Amir enthusiastically supported the idea and offered his help. The number and quality of the Hebrew sources cannot be felt outside of Israel due to language barriers, but as the extent of the proliferation of English language publications was captured, I set out to systematically identify these sources.

The search for this collection utilized journal indexes, bibliographical sources, data bases, authors' curriculum vitae and interviews with authors to cover as many sources as possible. The interested reader will find out that the material included here is very comprehensive as preference was given to include rather than exclude sources. Unlike the Hebrew source book of 1991 which included references to unpublished masters theses and doctoral dissertations, this bibliographical source book includes only articles, books, book chapters, and published reports.

Each reference appears in the book only once and it appears in the category that is thought to best describe the purpose and applicability of the reference. However, a reference may have relevance to more than one area, and the reader is advised to consult the subject index for additional applications. Also, the reader is advised to consult the key words and the annotations for reference content.

This bibliographical source book includes everything that was found written on Israeli criminal justice until 1993. Most of the publications in English started to appear in the early 1960s with the advent of social sciences in Israel. Criminal justice was defined here as an all-inclusive term for the understanding of crime causation as well as capturing societal reaction to crime such as legislation, jurisprudence, law enforcement and corrections. Furthermore, an attempt was made to include wider societal aspects considered relevant to the commission of crime and formal handling of it. For this purpose a typology has been developed according to what was available in the literature and what could stand alone as a category. Therefore, in addition to self-evident categories such as corrections, criminology, drug addiction, juvenile delinquency, and law, the reader may find other relevant sources in areas such as political violence or social stress.

It was decided to include references written on Israel by Israeli criminal justice (and other) scholars and non-Israelis alike. It is often the case that cooperation between Israeli and non-Israeli scholars is evident in an effort to produce material about Israel or scholarly material that pertains to theoretical and/or empirical issues related to other countries as well in a cross cultural or comparative scholarship. Also some material not on Israel was included if written by an Israeli author. Every effort was made to verify the accuracy of each reference entry that was found or identified so that the information published here will correctly and accurately reflect the source as it appeared in print.

All secondary sources (i.e., those not directly found in or through library sources) were verified against the original publication for accuracy. Only references that could be verified against a library source or against the original work were included here. In several instances when a source was not available in U.S. libraries, an attempt was made to corroborate it against a data base in Israel and if that was not available, authors were requested to provide copies of their work. It is assumed then that spelling of authors' names, titles of publications, reference sources, years, volumes, issues, page numbers, publication houses and other pertinent information is correct.[1] This careful verification process resulted in the exclusion of only a handful of unverifiable sources. The utmost attention was given to guarantee that the text will be error-free. However, if it is found that a publication has been omitted or that an entry contains some error(s), the careful reader is kindly requested to bring any corrections and/or additions to our attention so they can be properly included in a future update.[2]

This source book includes more than 820 entries of articles, books, book chapters and some annual and other professional reports. Entries are followed by a short annotation and by key words (marked as "KW" appearing in alphabetical order) to provide a brief description about the entries.[3] The book ends with an index that includes authors' names, periodicals, subjects composed from the key words, as well as some pertinent concepts and terminology that appear in the entries, the key words and/or the annotations.

What is offered here to the interested reader is the first compilation of references in the English language that highlights the contribution of Israeli social scientists to the

---

[1] This explains why some authors' names appear more than once in the index. Typically in the translation from a Hebrew name to the English spelling, the name may appear in several variations.

[2] Please direct all correspondence to:
Robert R. Friedmann, Ph.D.
Professor and Chair
Department of Criminal Justice
Georgia State University
P.O.Box 4018
Atlanta, GA 30302-4018

For errors found please cite the reference as it appears in the book (reference number and page number as it appears in the book) and below it the correction(s) that need to be made. Please ascertain that names, titles, sources, page numbers and any other pertinent information are accurate. It would be most valuable to have a photocopy of the source included. If you wish to draw attention to material not included in this book, please send a copy of the article or chapter (if a book, send copy of all cover pages and table of contents). Only documented additions will be considered.

[3] Most entries are followed by a brief annotation. However, when a copy of an entry was not available, a minimal set of helpful key words has been provided.

general literature in criminal justice.[4] This most extensive empirical and theoretical body of knowledge exemplifies the interest of Israeli scientists in contributing to the general body of knowledge in criminal justice, often using the empirical findings from Israel to test and develop theories in the field. There is perhaps no other country with so small a number of criminal justice scholars, that has produced so many empirical and non-empirical research publications, or has generated interest in it as a social science and legal laboratory, as Israel.

It is hoped that this source book will be useful to scholars in Israel and those outside Israel who may be interested in comparative criminal justice. The wealth of reference sources here should aid scholars, students and professionals in criminal justice and related fields in their research and areas of professional interest. Some of the material compiled here has a quality second to none. The contributions of Israeli scholars add a comparative dimension to criminal justice knowledge as well as a direct contribution to its core.

No attempt was made at this stage to provide a "sociology of criminal justice" here, but even in a cursory look it becomes rather evident that some areas in criminal justice have received more disproportional (large or small) attention than might be expected. For example, great interest has been placed on research into drug use and alcohol consumption despite the fact that Israel was not known (at least in the days preceding this research) as a substance abuse society. On the other hand, the absence of much research on formal social control and particularly on law enforcement is almost striking. Israel has a relatively large centralized police force that is occupied with public safety as well as internal security, yet the dearth of research in this area raises a question of why there was insufficient interest on the part of scientists (and grantors of funds). Of course, similar observations to the one above could (and perhaps should) be made into other areas of criminal justice in Israel. Some research is intriguing, such as that on political violence as it is associated with nation building; others seem relevant to the occurrence of crime and the particulars of Israeli society, such as stress. The topics, content areas, types of research and its quality and saliency ought to stimulate the interest of and be of value to those who are doing research and writing in this field.

---

[4] As well as those non-Israelis who, for various intellectual and other reasons, found Israel interesting enough as a social laboratory to do their research there with (or without) Israeli colleagues.

Acknowledgments

No project of this kind is possible without the collaboration of many people who worked hard to make this idea become a reality. Those involved in this project should receive acknowledgement, and I would like to take this opportunity to recognize the contribution of those who made the painstaking task of assembling this source book less complicated and more enjoyable. First, Menachem Amir, of the Institute of Criminology at the Hebrew University in Jerusalem, was instrumental in his encouragement to proceed with this project and with the generous assistance and extensive support he provided. Richard Terrill, of Georgia State University, deserves thanks for his collegial guidance. Patricia Carrell, Dean of the College of Public and Urban Affairs at Georgia State University was most supportive at times when there were questions about whether this project would become a reality. Valrie Abrahams, also of Georgia State University, provided essential and dedicated assistance in the source verification process.

Ruth Teitelbaum, director of the Social Science Information Center at the Henrietta Szold Institute in Jerusalem, was instrumental in the verification of sources that could not be found in American libraries or even from authors. Her dedication, support, advice and tireless hard work made this international cooperation a pleasant and enjoyable experience and allowed completion of this source book.

Thanks are also due to the Henrietta Szold Institute for its interest in this project and for its professional support. I would especially like to thank my Israeli colleagues who expressed their enthusiasm and were very cooperative and responsive at different stages of this project. Simha Landau, of the Hebrew University, and Giora Rahav, of Tel-Aviv University, were particularly helpful. I greatly appreciate the interest that Greenwood Press has shown in this project and for the encouragement and guidance I received from my editor, Mildred Vasan. Finally, I wish to thank Liz Leiba and Jane Lerner at Greenwood Press and Amy Nease at Georgia State University for their help with proofing the manuscript.

Atlanta
August 1994

1

Addiction: Drugs and Alcohol

001 Adler, I. and D. B. Kandel. 1981. "Cross-Cultural Perspectives on Developmental Stages in Adolescent Drug Use." *Journal of Studies on Alcohol* 42(9):705-15.

KW: Adolescents / Alcohol use / Comparative research / Drug use

002 Adler, I. and D. B. Kandel. 1982. "A Cross-Cultural Comparison of Sociopsychological Factors in Alcohol Use Among Adolescents in Israel, France and the United States." *Journal of Youth and Adolescence* 11(2):89-113.

This study compares alcohol consumption in three countries, France, Israel and the United States. It examines independent variables such as demography, behaviors, attitudes, peers and parents. Parental and peer influences were found to be more important than the presence of a "youth subculture."

KW: Adolescents / Alcohol use / Comparative research / France / Peer groups / Social norms / United States

003 Adler, I. and D. B. Kandel. 1983. "Risk Periods for Drug Involvement in Adolescence in France and in Israel: Application of Survival Analysis to Cross-Sectional Data." *Social Forces* 62(2):375-97.

This study identifies potential periods when there is greater likelihood or risk for using legal and illicit drugs. Different patterns were found for Israel and France. The higher the availability of a drug the higher the likelihood of use at early age.

KW: Adolescents / Alcohol use / Comparative research / Drug use / France / Sex differences / Smoking

004 Amir, M. 1980. "Israel." Pp. 171-98 in *The Community's Response to Drug Use*, edited by S. Einstein. New York: Pergamon Press.

Attributes the seriousness of Israel's drug problem to the following trends: Transition from endemic to epidemic proportions, changes in social characteristics of drug abusers, changes in the types of drugs used, the types of offenses connected with addiction, development of specialized underworld, drugs became a security problem, drugs are part of international networks, and changes in the public and government perception of the drug abuse problem.

KW: Drug addiction / Drug use

005 Amir, M. and P. Eldar. 1979. "An Experiment in the Treatment of Alcoholics in Israel." *Drug Forum* 7(2):105-19.

This treatment project is comprised of the following six phases: identifying the alcoholics, tailoring a personal treatment, avoidance, rehabilitation, integration, internal leadership and follow-up.

KW: Alcohol withdrawal / Alcoholism / Intervention programs

006 Barnea, Z. 1989. "A Critical and Comparative Review of the Prevention of Drug and Alcohol Abuse in Israel." *Journal of Drug Education* 19(1):59-81.

This study is a survey of the different intervention programs and strategies for prevention of addiction to alcohol and drugs. Focus is on primary and secondary prevention. Prevention programs did not reach at-risk populations.

KW: Alcoholism / Drug use / Intervention programs / Literature review / Population at risk / Prevention

007 Barnea, Z., G. Rahav and M. Teichman. 1987. "The Reliability and Consistency of Self Reports on Substance Use in A Longitudinal Study." *British Journal of Addictions* 82(8): 891-8.

This study is an assessment of the stability and consistency of adolescents' self-reports on drug abuse. Findings indicated a great level of stability and consistency across time.

KW: Adolescents / Drug addiction / Longitudinal study

008 Barnea, Z., G. Rahav and M. Teichman. 1992. "Personality, Cognitive and Interpersonal Factors in Adolescent Substance Use: A Longitudinal Test of An Integrative Model." *Journal of Youth and Adolescence* 21(2):187-202.

Examines a multi-dimensional model to explain drug use by adolescents. Cognitive and interpersonal variables were found influential. Sensation seeking was important but anxiety, depression and socio-demographic variables did not have an influence on drug use and neither did the availability of drugs.

KW: Adolescents / Demographic traits / Drug use / Interpersonal relations / Needs / Personality traits

009 Barnea, Z., M. Teichman, and G. Rahav. 1992. "Alcohol Consumption Among Israeli Youth - 1989: Epidemiology and Demographics." *British Journal of Addictions* 87:295-302.

KW: Adolescents / Alcohol use / Juvenile delinquency / Socioeconomic status / Students

010 Ben-Yehuda, N. 1987. "Drug Abuse Social Policy in the United States and Israel: A Comparative Sociological Perspective." *The International Journal of the Addictions* 22(1):17-45.

Presents a sociological perspective to view drug abuse as a moral-ideological problem, not a technical-medical one. The explanation focuses on the different cultural matrices of Israel and the U.S. Success in combating drug abuse in Israel was attributed to tighter closure of borders, military service and lesser individualism.

KW: Comparative research / Cultural differences / Drug use / Prevention / Social policy / United States

011 Bensinger, G. J. 1981. "Immune for Years, Israel Finds Drug Problem Under Its Skin." *Law Enforcement News* VII(19, November 9):3.

KW: Drug problem

012 Butler, E. W., S. Schuller-Friedman and D. Shichor. 1990. "Alcohol and Drug Use Among Impaired and Non-Impaired Elderly Persons." Pp. 163-90 in *The Socio-Cultural Matrix of Alcohol and Drug Use: A Sourcebook of Patterns and Factors,* edited by B. Forster and J. C. Salloway. Lewiston, NY: Edwin Mellen Press.

Examines several key questions about the drug use of the elderly by utilizing data from a general community sample of older people in a southern California medium-sized city. The study looks at the extent of drugs used by the elderly, including how many and what types of drugs were used. It also focuses on drug use differences by impaired as opposed to non-impaired older persons.

KW: Alcohol use / Drug use / Elderly / Impaired persons

013 Cromer, G. 1989. "The Response of Ultra-Orthodox Judaism to the Problem of Drug Use: A Case Study and Its Implications." *Violence, Aggression and Terrorism* 3(3):191-202.

Discusses the rhetoric of the Jewish orthodoxy against drug use as a private case of using a social problem as a base of attack against secular society by presenting social problems as symptomatic of failures.

KW: Cultural differences / Drug addiction / Drug use / Secular people / Ultra-orthodox Jews

014 Dauber, E. 1973. "Developing a Drug Policy: A Suggested Approach." *Israel Studies in Criminology* II:153-70.

KW: Drug use / Social policy

015 Ehrenfeld, R. and L. Sebba. 1991. "Involuntary Treatment of Drug Addicts in Israel." In *The Compulsory Treatment of Opiate Dependence*, edited by W. H. McGlothlin and D. Anglin. Binghamton: Haworth.

Discusses the problem of compulsory treatment of drug users, the classification of drug addiction as a conventional mental disorder, and the fusion of punishment and treatment.

KW: Drug addiction / Drug rehabilitation

016 Einstein, S. 1989. *Drugs and Alcohol Use: Issues and Factors*. New York: Plenum Press.

A collection of articles based on papers presented at the first international conference on drug addiction. The papers offer theoretical and empirical programmatic efforts integrating theses, experiments and data. Discusses causes for addiction and support groups for intervention programs and services.

KW: Alcoholism / Drug addiction / Intervention programs

017 Fine, E. W., S. A. Richman, and M. Teichman. 1980. "Depression in Female Alcoholics." Pp. 447-53 in *Currents in Alcoholism*, Vol. 7, edited by M. Galanter. New York: Grune and Stratton.

This study reports the incidence, severity and characteristics of clinically significant depressive illness in 28 consecutive female admissions to an alcoholism inpatient unit in a community general hospital.

KW: Alcoholism / Depression / Women

018 Friedman, I. and I. Peer. 1970. "Drug Addiction Among Pimps and Prostitutes in Israel." *Israel Studies in Criminology* I:141-76.

KW: Drug addiction / Pimps / Prostitution

019 Hobfoll, S. E., T. Rom and B. Segal. 1989. "Sensation Seeking, Anxiety, and Risk Taking in the Israeli Context." Pp. 53-9 in *Drugs and Alcohol Use: Issues and Factors*, edited by S. Einstein. New York: Plenum Press.

Studying Israeli youth culture, it maintained that sensation seeking would be predictive of participation in high risk or stimulating behavior; that sensation seeking would be related to participation in special combat units of the armed services and to participation in risky and stimulating sports; and that those who indicated they used substances would be higher on a trait anxiety than nonusers, but that high trait-anxious persons would avoid dangerous sports and combat military participation.

KW: Alcohol use / Anxiety / Drug use / Risk taking / Sensation seeking

020 Jacobsen, C. and R. A. Hanneman. 1992. "Illegal Drugs: Past, Present, and Possible Futures." *Journal of Drug Issues* 22(1):105-20.

Following a long period of increase in drug use in the U.S., a sharp decrease was observable from 1980 and on. The study simulated a computerized model of drug use and showed a theory adoptable to drug use. Fear of AIDS was offered as best explanation.

KW: Drug use / Sociological theories / Statistical data / United States

021 Javetz, R. and J. T. Shuval. 1990. "Normative Contexts of Drug Use Among Israeli Youth." Pp. 427-59 in *The Socio-Cultural Matrix of Alcohol and Drug Use: A Sourcebook of Patterns and Factors,* edited by B. Forster and J. C. Salloway. Lewiston, NY: Edwin Mellen Press.

Analyzed the normative-motivational context of illicit drug use among high school students on the basis of a two-dimensional conceptual model: One dimension relates to levels of actions - attitudes about drug use and other deviant behavior and actual drug use; the other deals with the frames of reference - personal characteristics and attitudes attributed to others.

KW: Adolescents / Drug use / Social norms

022 Kandel, D. B. and I. Adler. 1982. "Socialization into Marijuana Use Among French Adolescents: A Cross-Cultural Comparison with the United States." *Journal of Health and Social Behavior* 23(4):295-309.

Examines the correlations and predictors of marijuana use among adolescents in France and the United States. French used less than Americans and peer use was found to be best predictor.

KW: Adolescents / Comparative research / Drug use / France / Marijuana / Socialization / United States

023 Kandel, D. B., I. Adler and M. Sudit. 1981. "The Epidemiology of Adolescent Drug Use in France and Israel." *American Journal of Public Health* 71(3):256-65.

Compared epidemiological data concerning drug use among adolescents in France and Israel to see whether drug use was influenced by heavy alcohol consumption. The heavy use of one drug (alcohol) pointed to a more permissive attitude towards the use of drugs in general.

KW: Adolescents / Alcohol use / Comparative research / Drug use / France / Permissive attitudes

024 Kandel, D. B., O. Simcha-Fagan and M. Davis. 1986. "Risk Factors for Delinquency and Illicit Drug Use from Adolescence to Young Adulthood." *Journal of Drug Issues* 16(1):67-90.

KW: Adolescents / Drug use / Juvenile delinquency / Risk factors / Young adults

025 Landau, S. F. and I. Drapkin. 1966. "Drug Offenders in Israel." *British Journal of Criminology* 6:376-90.

KW: Drug use / Juvenile delinquency

026 Lison, S., R. Saenger and I. Vinder. 1989. "Stages in the Multifaceted Treatment of the Multiproblem Drug Abuser." Pp. 155-62 in *Drugs and Alcohol Use: Issues and Factors*, edited by S. Einstein. New York: Plenum Press.

Describes a program where a wide range of coordinated therapeutic interventions were applied over a period of time by a network of professionals in various settings and agencies. The caseworker or therapist from the primary drug-treatment facility was responsible for the treatment program. Emphasis was given to the multifaceted therapeutic process.

KW: Drug addiction / Drug rehabilitation / Therapy

027 Peled, T. and H. Schimmerling. 1973. "The Drug Culture among the Youth of Israel: The Case of High School Students." *Israel Studies in Criminology* II:125-52.

KW: Adolescents / Drug use / High schools / Youth culture

028 Richman, S. A., M. Teichman, and E. W. Fine. 1980. "Psychological Differences Between Male and Female Alcoholics." Pp. 497-502 in *Currents in Alcoholism*, Vol. 7, edited by M. Galanter. New York: Grune and Stratton.

This study was designed to further explore and compare psychological characteristics in male and female alcoholics at an inpatient treatment program of an urban general hospital. In addition to comparing male and female variables, the study also attempted to determine whether there was any correlation between depression and female alcoholics.

KW: Alcoholism / Psychological differences / Sex differences / Treatment

029 Rivlin, E. 1976. "Psychological Aspects of the Use of Drugs in the Youth Counter-Culture." Pp. 159-71 in *Youth Unrest*, edited by S. G. Shoham. Jerusalem: Jerusalem Academic Press.

Portrays an anti-intellectual, anti-ideological youth movement, largely chaotic in nature, in which many made their entrances and exits, with no unified world outlook, and with de-emphasis with respect to rational understanding.

KW: Adolescents / Drug use / Youth culture

030 Sebba, L. and R. Ehrenfeld. 1982. "Compulsory Treatment for Drug Offenders Under Israeli Law: A Research Note." *Medicine and Law* 1:109-11.

Discusses the problem of compulsory treatment of drug users, the classification of drug addiction as a conventional mental disorder, and the fusion of punishment and treatment.

KW: Drug addiction / Drug rehabilitation

031 Shoham, S. G., I. Baruch, G. Rahav, R. Markowski, F. Chard and M. Ben-Haim. 1984. "Personality Core Dynamics and Drug Preference." Drug and Alcohol Dependence 13(3):297-303.

Examines the relationships between personality variables and personality types of addicts to hard drugs in an attempt to ascertain an assumption about differential addiction patterns.

KW: Drug addiction / Personality traits / Psychological theories

032 Shoham, S. G., N. Geva, D. Kliger and T. Chai. 1974. "Drug Abuse Among Israeli Youth: Epidemiological Pilot Study." *Bulletin of Narcotics* 26(2):9-28. Also published in *Israel Studies in Criminology* III:97-146, 1976.

Attempted to define relationships between knowledge, techniques and attitudes towards use of drugs and demographic characteristics. Legitimacy, or lack of it, for drug use was a key factor influencing drug abuse while demand, supply and techniques were secondary in importance.

KW: Addiction / Adolescents / Attitudes / Drug use / Epidemiology

033 Shoham, S. G., G. Rahav, Y. Esformes, J. Blau, N. Kaplinsky, R. Markovski and B. Wolf. 1978. "Differential Patterns of Drug Involvement Among Israeli Youth." *Bulletin of Narcotics* 30(4):17-32.

Describes drug using juveniles in comparison to non-drug using juveniles in an attempt to examine which demographic, attitudinal and socioeconomic variables influenced drug use. Most users were low socioeconomic class dropouts.

KW: Adolescents / Drug use / Family relations / Socioeconomic status

034 Shoham, S. G., G. Rahav, Y. Esformes, J. Blau, N. Kaplinsky, R. Markovsky and B. Wolf. 1981. "Polar Types of Reported Drug Involvement Among Israeli Youth." *International Journal of the Addictions* 16(7):1161-7.

This is the third study in the series. It attempted to describe different types of adolescents using drugs and the distinguishing parameters among them. Drug use appeared most frequent among youth with low parental supervision.

KW: Adolescents / Drug use / Involvement / Parent-child relations / Socioeconomic status

035 Shoham, S. G., G. Rahav, Y. Esformes, J. Blau, N. Kaplinsky, R. Markovsky, B. Wolf and F. Chard. 1986. "Drug and Alcohol Involvement Among Israeli Youth." *Israel Studies in Criminology* VII:54-87. Also published as Shoham, S. G., pp. 197-228, in *Mentally Abnormal and Drug Addicted Offenders*, edited by W. T. Haesler. Diessenhofen, verlag Ruegger. 1984.

This study found that drug users were adolescents from low socioeconomic status who dropped out of school and found peers who compensated them for unstable family relations and lack of involvement in school. Those from higher socioeconomic status sought emotional experience.

KW: Adolescents / Alcohol use / Drug use / Family relations / Involvement / Socioeconomic status

036 Shoham, S. G., G. Rahav, Y. Esformes, R. Markovski, F. Chard and N. Kaplinsky. 1980. "Some Parameters of the Use of Alcohol by Israeli Youth and Its Relationship to their Involvement with Cannabis and Tobacco." *Drug and Alcohol Dependence* 6:263-72.

Describes general trends in alcohol use and profiles of drinkers. Examines the relationship between drinking and smoking and using Hashish. Higher rate of alcohol consumption was reported on delinquent youth and those with adolescence problems without parental supervision.

KW: Adolescents / Alcohol use / Drug use / Involvement / Smoking / Parent-child relations / Youth in distress

037 Simcha-Fagan, O., J. C. Gersten and T. S. Langner. 1986. "Early Precursors and Concurrent Correlates of Patterns of Illicit Drug Use in Adolescence." *Journal of Drug Issues* 16(1):7-28.

KW: Adolescents / Drug use

038 Teichman, M. 1981. "State-Trait Anxiety in Methadone Maintenance Patients." *The International Journal of the Addictions* 16:1125-8.

Examines the impact of daily methadone consumption on situational and trait anxiety of recovering substance users. The daily dose reduced the situational anxiety but not trait anxiety.

KW: Anxiety / Drug rehabilitation / Methadone / Personality traits

039 Teichman, M. 1986. "A Relapse Inoculation Training for Recovering Alcoholics." *Alcoholism Treatment Quarterly* 3(4):133-9.

Describes a treatment program for recovered alcoholics and drug users who underwent a relapse. The program was based on theoretical elements that attempted to explain the return to substance use and the treatment process that was based on several long term stages.

KW: Alcohol rehabilitation / Alcoholism / Drug addiction

040 Teichman, M. 1989. "Dealing With the Relapse: A Relapse Inoculation Training Program." Pp. 209-14 in *Drugs and Alcohol Use: Issues and Factors*, edited by S. Einstein. New York: Plenum Press.

Describes a treatment program for recovered alcoholics and drug users who underwent a relapse. The program was based on Marlatt's theoretical elements of abstinence violation effect that attempted to explain the return to substance use. The treatment process was based on several long term stages.

KW: Alcohol rehabilitation / Alcoholism / Group work

041 Teichman, M., Z. Barnea, and G. Rahav. 1987. "Alcohol Consumption among Israeli Adolescents: A Decade of Research. *Israel Journal of Psychiatry and Related Sciences* 24(4):281-8.

A survey of research and epidemiological reviews between 1976 and 1986 on changes in alcohol consumption among Israeli adolescents. Age and gender impacted alcohol consumption and so did the father's ethnic origin. Consumption was higher among "external" high school students.

KW: Adolescents / Age differences / Alcohol use / Gender differences / Literature review

042 Teichman, M., Z. Barnea and G. Rahav. 1987. "Alcohol and Psychoactive Drug Use Among Israeli Adolescents: An Epidemiological and Demographic Investigation." *International Journal of the Addictions* 22(1):81-92.

This is a study on the epidemiology and demography of alcohol and drug use among youth in Israel. Data indicated a slight increase in use among youth and that there was a relation between frequency of consumption and gender and age.

KW: Adolescents / Age differences / Alcohol use / Drug use / Gender differences / Socioeconomic status

043 Teichman, M., Z. Barnea and G. Rahav. 1989. "Personality and Psychoactive Substance Use Among Adolescents: A Longitudinal Study." *British Journal of Addictions* 84(2):181-90.

Explores the influence that sensation seeking, depression and propensity for depression had on starting to use or continuing to use drugs. Sensation seeking had a stronger impact than depression as did prior experience.

KW: Adolescents / Anxiety / Crime causes / Depression / Drug use / Longitudinal study

044 Teichman, M., Z. Barnea and G. Rahav. 1989. "Sensation Seeking, State and Trait Anxiety, and Depressive Mood in Adolescent Substance Users." *International Journal of the Addictions* 24(2):87-99.

Explores the extent to which sensation seeking, depression, propensity for depression, anxiety and availability of drugs influenced narcotic intake (drug and alcohol use) among adolescents. Sensation seeking had a stronger impact than depression as did prior experience and availability of narcotics.

KW: Adolescents / Anxiety / Depression / Drug use / Sensation seeking

045 Teichman, M., G. Rahav, and Z. Barnea. 1988. "A Comprehensive Substance Prevention Program: An Israeli Experiment." *Journal of Alcohol and Drug Education* 33(3):1-10.

This study discusses a proposed plan to prevent drug and alcohol use among Israeli youth. Authors assumed that substance use increased with positive attitudes towards use and if these attitudes were reinforced by parents and peers who were users.

KW: Adolescents / Alcohol use / Drug use / Intervention programs / Prevention

046 Teichman, M., G. Rahav and Z. Barnea. 1990. "Prevention and Treatment of Alcohol and Drug Abuse." Pp. 460-84 in *The Sociocultural Matrix of Alcohol and Drug Use: A Sourcebook of Patterns and Factors,* edited by B. Forster and J. C. Salloway. Lewiston, NY: Edwin Mellen Press.

KW: Alcohol rehabilitation / Alcoholism / Drug addiction / Drug rehabilitation / Prevention / Treatment

047 Teichman, M., G. Rahav, and Z. Barnea. 1990. "A Multi-Dimensional Model of Psychoactive Substance Use by Israeli Adolescents." Pp. 461-84 in *The Socio-Cultural Matrix of Alcohol and Drug Use: A Sourcebook of Patterns and Factors*, edited by B. Forster and J. C. Salloway. Lewiston, NY: Edwin Mellen Press.

Presents a multi-dimensional model of juvenile drug and alcohol use that includes such variables as personality, cognitive process, interpersonal and intersocial factors and access to drugs and alcohol in the community. Also presents a prevention program based on the model and other findings.

KW: Adolescents / Alcohol use / Attitudes / Drug use / Intervention programs / Models / Personality traits / Prevention

048 Teichman, M., S. Richman, and E. W. Fine. 1987. "Dose/Duration Effect Relation Between Alcohol Consumption and Cerebral Atrophy: A Psychological and Neuroradiological Evaluation." *American Journal of Drug and Alcohol Abuse* 13(3):357-63. Also published as "Cerebral Atrophy in Chronic Alcoholic Patients." Pp. 357-62 in *Drugs and Alcohol Use: Issues and Factors*, edited by S. Einstein. New York: Plenum Press, 1989.

Observed cerebral atrophy in alcoholic patients focusing on the amount of alcohol consumed, length of consumption period, psychological and radiological methods of damage assessment. CAT SCAN and MFD indicated severe damage, psychological and radiological measures were highly correlated, and a high correlation appeared between length of consumption and quantity.

KW: Alcoholism / Brain damage / Neuropsychology

049 Teichman, M. and Y. Teichman. 1987. "Perceived Need for Interpersonal Resources in Three Developmental Stages: Adolescence, Young Adulthood and Adulthood." *Israel Journal of Psychiatry and Related Sciences* 24(3):167-78. Also published by Teichman, Y. and M. Teichman as "Perceived Need for Interpersonal Resources by Israeli Drug Abusers." *The International Journal of the Addictions* 24(4):325-35, 1989.

Explores perceived need for interpersonal resources in three stages: adolescents, young adults, and adults, based on Erikson's theory. Adolescents and adults were found to have similar needs for resources.

KW: Adolescents / Adults / Developmental stages / Drug addiction / Interpersonal relations / Psychological needs / Young adults

050 Teichman, Y. and M. Teichman. 1990. "Interpersonal View of Depression: Review and Integration." *Journal of Family Psychology* 3(4):349-67.

A review of three interpersonal models of depression as stemming from interaction between the depressed and their significant others. Treatment was based on the concept of reciprocity in depression.

KW: Depression / Family relations / Interpersonal relations / Literature review / Treatment methods

051 Teichman, M., Y. Teichman, and Z. Barnea. 1988. "Prevention of Adolescents Substance Use: A Description of a Parental Involvement Program." *Special Services in the Schools* 5(1-2):89-96.

Describes a drug and alcohol prevention program that involved parents in education, treatment and counseling within a school framework. Background and training workshop were also offered.

KW: Adolescents / Alcohol use / Drug use / Intervention programs / Parent-child relationship / Parent participation / Prevention

052 Teichman, M., Y. Teichman, J. Converse, and U. G. Foa. 1992. "The Interpersonal Needs of Drug Addicts: Are They Similar Across Cultures?" *The International Journal of the Addictions* 27:281-8.

Examines the need for interpersonal resources of drug addicts in Israel and the U.S. as compared to normal subjects. Differences were found between the two groups within the two countries but similarities were found between drug addicts in both.

KW: Comparative research / Cultural differences / Drug addiction / Interpersonal relations / Psychological needs / United States

2

Corrections and Probation

053 Amir, M. 1966. "Sociological Study of the House of Correction (Prison)." *American Journal of Correction* 28(2):20-4.

KW: Prisons

054 Amir, M. 1969. "Personnel Recruitment in Correction." Pp. 224-43 in *Scripta Hierosolymitana*, Vol. 21, *Studies in Criminology*, edited by I. Drapkin. Jerusalem: The Magnes Press, The Hebrew University.

KW: Personnel recruitment (corrections)

055 Ben-David, S. 1992. "Staff-to-Inmates Relations in a Total Institution: A Model of Five Modes of Association." *International Journal of Offender Therapy and Comparative Criminology* 36(3):209-19.

Examines the relations system between prisoners and guards in prison. Identified five types of relations: penalizing, controlling, patronizing, therapeutic, and integrative. They were distinguished by the social distance between prisoner and guard. This contradicted Goffman's theory where relations in total institutions are inevitably hostile.

KW: Interpersonal relations / Prison guards / Prisoners / Prisons / Psychiatry / Total institutions

056 Bensinger, G. J. 1981. "Probation in Israel: An International Perspective." *Journal of Probation and Parole* 13:1-6.

Describes the historical development of the probation system in Israel from its pre-state situation during the British Mandate in Palestine to the end of the 1970s.

KW: Historical research / Probation

057 Bensinger, G. J. 1983. "Prisons in Israel." *Corrections Today* 45(5):56-8; 66-7.

Discusses the problems facing the correctional system in Israel in light of a panel's report that concluded that conditions in Israeli prisons were serious, subhuman and on the verge of explosion.

KW: Corrections / Overcrowding / Prisons

058 Bensinger, G. J. 1984. "Corrections in Israel and the United States: A Comparative Analysis." *International Journal of Comparative and Applied Criminal Justice* 8(1):55-62. Also published in *Prisons Around the World: Studies in International Penology*, edited by M. R. Carlie and K. I. Minor. Dubuque, IA: Wm. C. Brown, 1992.

The departure point for this study was that the general underlying philosophical intent of corrections in both Israel and the United States was the restoration of the offender to a productive role in the community. Focus is on two correctional alternatives: incarceration and probation. The author argues that probation in Israel was not considered a punishment but was part of general social services. Maintains that corrections has not been a priority in Israel and that it needs to be re-examined.

KW: Comparative research / Incarceration / Probation / United States

059 Bensinger, G. J. and M. Seng. 1986. "Probation in Illinois: Some New Directions." *Federal Probation* 50(3):66-73.

Describes several interrelated factors that were identified as having an important impact in achieving meaningful probation in Illinois Corrections. These were prison crowding, LEAA-initiated change, legislative developments and trends in felony probation.

KW: Probation / United States

060 Carmi, A. 1978. "The Challenge of Experimentation." Pp. 1-14 in *Medical Experimentation*, edited by A. Carmi. Ramat-Gan, Israel: Turtledove Publishing.

This study argues that experimentation needs control in the political-economic aspect and the normative, legal, and ethical one.

KW: Experiment

061 Cavior, H. E. and S. Cohen. 1975. "Evaluation Research: Perspectives from a Corrections Setting." *Criminal Justice and Behavior* 2(3):237-57.

KW: Correctional rehabilitation / Evaluation research

062 Cavior, H. E. and S. Cohen. 1979. "The Development of a Scale to Assess Inmate and Staff Attitude towards Co-Corrections." *Human Organization* 38(1):12-19.

KW: Attitudes / Co-corrections / Prison guards / Prisoners

063 Cohen, B-Z., R. Eden and A. Lazar. 1991. "The Efficacy of Probation Versus Imprisonment in Reducing Recidivism of Serious Offenders in Israel." *Journal of Criminal Justice* 19:263-70.

Examines the impact of imprisonment and probation on criminal recidivism. No significant differences were found. Lack of education was a far better predictor of recidivism than sentencing.

KW: Crime / Demographic characteristics / Education level / Predisposition / Prisoners / Probation / Recidivism

064 Cohen, S. 1972. "Writing from Inside." *New Society* 31 (August):447-9.
Presents prison literature (written by inmates) as falling into three categories: The first originated with those prisoners who entered the system because of offenses generally accepted as ideological, the second category became politically minded in prison itself, and the third category came from all other prisoners who managed to write and be published (even when not politically motivated).

KW: Prisoners / Prisons / United Kingdom

065 Cohen, S. 1974. "Human Warehouses: The Future of Our Prisons?" *New Society* 14 (November):407-11.
Cohen asks: If prison becomes more and more a punishment only for the worst offenders, what follows? Segregation within an inhuman system of Chinese boxes? He argues that in the future, penal systems would look like human warehouses with people stored indefinitely. He expects reactions by public opinion, prisoners' unions and by prisoners themselves.

KW: Prisons / United Kingdom

066 Cohen, S. 1977. "Introduction and Commentary, 'Notes on the Reformation of a Criminal.'" in *Angel Face: the Making of a Criminal*, by W. Probyn. Pp. 11-17; 232-54, Boston: George Allen and Unwin.
Discusses the relevance of the private experience of a long-term inmate to the public issue of imprisonment.

KW: Criminals / Prisons / United Kingdom

067 Cohen, S. 1977. "Prisons and the Future of Control Systems: From Concentration to Dispersal." Pp. 217-28 in *Welfare in Action*, edited by M. Fitzgerald, P. Halmos, J. Muncie and D. Zeldin. London: Routledge & Kegan Paul in association with The Open University Press.
Constructed a scenario based on extrapolations from current developments in the prison systems of the advanced industrial societies of the West, particularly America and Britain. All these predictions assumed that it was possible to learn from the past.

KW: Prisons / United Kingdom / United States

068 Cohen, S. 1982. *Angel Face.* New York: St. Martin's Press.

KW: Criminals / Prisons

069 Cohen, S. 1982. "Western Crime Control Models in the Third World: Benign or Malignant?" *Research in Law, Deviance and Social Control* 4:85-119.

Presents a classification of various crime control models in western countries. Cohen examines the applicability of this classification to the third world. Crime was perceived as inevitable; three models were offered and critiqued.

KW: Crime / Crime prevention / Developing countries / International relations / Models / Western countries

070 Cohen, S. 1983. "Social Control Talk: Telling Stories About Correctional Change." In *The Power to Punish*, edited by P. Young and D. Garland. Atlantic Highlands, NJ: Humanities Press.

Discusses theories and views on social control in general and crime and delinquency control in particular. Also deals with the relationship between them and reality. Reviews the concepts of community, minimal statism and new behaviorism.

KW: Corrections / Crime / Delinquency prevention / Social control / Sociological theories

071 Cohen, S. and L. Taylor. 1971. "The Closed Emotional World of the Security Prison." *New Edinburgh Review*, November:4-8.

Using "new" criminology, this study examines how men who faced up to 25 years in prison came to terms with their predicament. The authors inquire into the ways in which such men experienced time, how they divided it and how they made it pass.

KW: Prisoners / Prisons

072 Cohen, S. and L. Taylor. 1972. *Psychological Survival: The Experience of Long Term Imprisonment*. Baltimore, MD: Penguin. Also published in second and revised edition, 1981.

This book is on the experience of long term imprisonment and its psychological impact on prisoners. The book discusses the psychological deterioration of prisoners, their reaction to emotional disturbance and their adjustment to prison conditions. It also discusses personal identity in prison and issues of authority and solidarity.

KW: Emotional responses / Mental disorders / Prisons / Prisoners / Self-concept / Social adjustment

073 Cohen, S. and L. Taylor. 1975. "Prison Research: A Cautionary Tale." *New Society* 30 (January):253-5.

Provides an account on how official resistance to penal research "killed" the planned research project. This resistance was not done abruptly but was carried over seven years on seemingly small matters.

KW: Prisons / Research

074 Cohen, S. and L. Taylor. 1977. "Talking About Prison Blues." Pp. 67-86 in *Doing Sociological Research*, edited by C. Bell and H. Newby. New York:

Free Press.

KW: Prison guards / Research

075 Di Gennaro, G. and E. Vetere. 1976. "Prison Resocialization at a Crossroad." *Israel Studies in Criminology* III:220-50.

KW: Prisons / Socialization

076 Eaton, J. W. and M. Amir. 1966. "Manpower Strategy in the Correctional Field." Pp. 71-97 in *Manpower and Training for Corrections*, edited by C. S. Prigmore. New York: Council on Social Work Education.

Suggests that professional planning in the corrections field requires specialized education, domestic service utilization, correctional reform, and matching fund subsidies.

KW: Personnel / Prisons

077 Eisikovits, Z. and E. Guttman. 1986. "Being in Nothingness: The Adolescent Experience in Prison." Pp. 219-38 in *People in Institutions: The Israeli Scene,* edited by Y. Kashti and M. Arieli. London: Freund Publishing House.

Discusses the adolescent's prison experience focusing on time perception, space perception and the perception of others.

KW: Adolescents / Juvenile delinquency / Prisons / Social perception / Space perception / Time perception

078 Erez, E. 1985. "Random Assignment, the Least Fair of Them All: Prisoners' Attitudes Toward Various Criteria of Selection." *Criminology* 23(2):365-79.

KW: Attitudes / Prisoners

079 Erez, E. 1986. "Randomized Experiments in Correctional Context: Legal, Ethical and Practical Concerns." *Journal of Criminal Justice* 14(5):401-12.

KW: Corrections / Ethics / Experiment

080 Erez, E. 1989. "Gender, Rehabilitation and Probation Decisions." *Criminology* 27(2):307-27.

KW: Correctional rehabilitation / Gender differences / Probation

081 Erez, E. 1992. "Dangerous Men, Evil Women: Gender and Parole Decision Making." *Justice Quarterly* 9(1):105-26.

KW: Gender differences / Parole / Prisoners

082 Frishtik, M. 1988. "The Probation Officer's Recommendation in His 'Investigation Report.'" *Journal of Offender Counseling, Services & Rehabilitation* 13(1):101-32.

Examines the considerations of probation officers when they recommend probation as opposed to rehabilitation. Probation officers were found to be influenced by a legalistic orientation and by the legal attitudes of the judges in their cases.

KW: Probation officer / Sentencing

083 Greenberg, O. 1986. "Exchange Relations Within Prison Walls." Pp. 167-80 in *People in Institutions: The Israeli Scene,* edited by Y. Kashti and M. Arieli. London: Freund Publishing House.

Examines the influence of social networks on inmate membership circles. Explained behavior of female inmates as based on interaction between inmates and guards and among inmates. Each inmate was part of several social networks that she created.

KW: Prison guards / Prisoners / Prisons / Social behavior / Social networks / Women

084 Hassin, Y. 1977. "Prisoners' Furlough: A Reassessment." *International Journal of Criminology and Penology* 5(3):171-8.

Examines furlough policy and the extent that furlough goals were achieved. Argues that policy objectives have not been achieved by furloughs.

KW: Furlough / Prisoners / Prisons

085 Hassin, Y. 1979. "The Prisoner's Family in Israel: Problems and Dilemmas." *International Social Work* 22(2):9-16.

Furloughs given after the second trimester of incarceration had no impact on improvement of family relations. Prisoners' wives became more dependent on social services than did prisoners' families.

KW: Family relations / Prisoners / Standard of living / Welfare recipients

086 Hassin, Y. 1980. "Early Release Committee for Prisoners v. Computer: Which is Preferable?" *Criminology* 18(3):385-97.

Attempted to identify the variables that might predict future criminal behavior of pre-release prisoners, in accordance with the criteria used by the release committee. Computer-generated recommendations were found to be more accurate than those made by the committee, particularly for predisposed prisoners.

KW: Behavior prediction / Computers / Predisposition / Prisoners / Prisoners' rehabilitation

087 Hassin, Y., 1986. "Early Release of Israeli Prisoners - Failure or Success?" *Israel Studies in Criminology* VII:177-95.

Examines the functioning of the committee for early release and assesses its success. Reports a high percentage of error in predicting successful integration of the released prisoner in the community.

KW: Early release / Prisoners / Rehabilitation / Sentencing

088 Hassin, Y. 1986. "Two Models for Predicting Recidivism: Clinical Versus Statistical - Another View." *The British Journal of Criminology* 26(3):270-86.
Studied the efficiency of two measures to predict behavior of prisoners on early release, that of the pardon board and a statistical prediction based on discriminant analysis. For recidivism, the computer model was more efficient and reliable.

KW: Behavior prediction / Computer model / Early release / Pardon / Prisoners / Recidivism

089 Hassin, Y. 1987. "Career Criminals, Recidivists and Dangerous Offenders: Distinguishing Groups of Offenders." *International Annals of Criminology* 25:233-51.

KW: Career criminals / Prisoners / Recidivism

090 Hoffman, A. 1990. "The Prisoner Rehabilitation Authority in Israel." Pp. 94-7 in *The Prevention of Crime and the Treatment of Offenders in Israel*, edited by Y. Tzubery, A Report to the Eighth UN Congress on the Prevention of Crime and the Treatment of Offenders, Havana, August 27 to September 7. Jerusalem: Ministry of Police.
Introduces a program developed by the Israel Prisoner Rehabilitation Authority. It was interdisciplinary, based on the idea of creating a new society - cutting the offenders off from their environment and providing for a new, non-criminal way of life.

KW: Crime prevention / Prisoner Rehabilitation Authority

091 Horovitz, M. 1965. "Probation in Israel." Pp. 106-21 in *The Prevention of Crime and the Treatment of Offenders in Israel*, A Report to the Third UN Congress on the Prevention of Crime and the Treatment of Offenders, Stockholm, August 9 to 18, Jerusalem, Israel: Government Printer.

KW: Probation

092 Hovav, M. 1990. "Supplement to Progress Report." Pp. 37-45 in *The Prevention of Crime and the Treatment of Offenders in Israel*, edited by Y. Tzubery, A Report to the Eighth UN Congress on the Prevention of Crime and the Treatment of Offenders, Havana, August 27 to September 7. Jerusalem: Ministry of Police.
This is a continuation of the summary of the Ministry of Police (1989) by presenting innovations in prevention and treatment of crime for a perspective of rehabilitation through employment and community activity.

KW: Crime prevention / Prisoners' rehabilitation

093 Hovav, M. 1990. "Alternatives to Imprisonment in Israel." Pp. 98-104 in *The Prevention of Crime and the Treatment of Offenders in Israel*, edited by Y.

Tzubery, A Report to the Eighth UN Congress on the Prevention of Crime and the Treatment of Offenders, Havana, August 27 to September 7. Jerusalem: Ministry of Police.

Focuses on several imprisonment alternatives: allowing offenders to stay in their natural surroundings with treatment incorporated therein (court-ordered probation, community service, electronic monitoring); allowing offenders to stay in their natural surroundings and changing occupational activities (service work, day centers); and moving offenders to other residential surroundings (residential facility, hostel).

KW: Alternatives to imprisonment

094 Israel Prison Service. 1993. *Annual Report: 1992/93*. Jerusalem: P.O.Box 2495.

KW: Prison services / Prisons / Statistics

095 Landau, S. F. 1969. "The Effect of Length of Imprisonment and Subjective Distance from Release on Future Time Perspective and Time Estimation of Prisoners." *Scripta Hierosolymitana* 21:182-223, *Studies in Criminology*, edited by I. Drapkin. Jerusalem: Magnes Press, The Hebrew University.

Aimed to find out (1) whether there was a relationship between Future Time Perspective (FTP) and time estimation, (2) how length of imprisonment and distance from release influenced these two variables in prisoners, and (3) the possible effect of other factors on FTP and time estimation and on the relationship between these two types of variables.

KW: Future time perspective / Prisoners

096 Lowenstein, A. 1984. "Coping With Stress: The Case of Prisoners' Wives." *Journal of Marriage and the Family* 46(3):699-708.

Examines coping needs of prisoners' wives and the factors that influenced those needs. Found eight coping styles for vulnerability in three areas. Successful coping depended on educational level, equal sharing in tasks and husband's sentence length.

KW: Coping behavior / Marital relations / Prisoners / Stress situations / Women

097 Lowenstein, A. 1986. "Temporary Single Parenthood - The Case of Prisoners' Families." *Family Relations* 35(1):79-85.

Examines the variables that influenced the adjustment of children to imprisoned fathers. A high percentage of children suffered emotional stress and their adjustment depended on personality and family variables of the mother such as age, family solidarity and quality of marriage.

KW: Emotional adjustment / Family relations / Prisoners / Single-parent families / Stress

098 Lowenstein, A. 1987. "Coping and Well-Being in 'Temporary' Single-Parent Families: The Case of Prisoners' Families." Pp. 147-56 in *Alternative Patterns*

of Family Life in Modern Societies, edited by L. Shamgar-Handelman and R. Palomba. Rome: National Institute for Population Research.

Assesses coping behavior of temporary single parent families with the (temporary) loss of the father/husband and its impact on their quality of life. The longer the separation the stronger the impact on physical and mental health of the wife and the children.

KW: Coping behavior / Family relations / Prisoners / Single-parent families / Women

099 McAfee, W. M. and D. Shichor. 1990. "A Historical-Sociological Analysis of California's Private Prison Experience in the 1850s: Some Modern Implications." *Criminal Justice History* XI:89-103.

Argues that the one historical example from over a century ago does not necessarily prove that privatization of maximum-security prisons must inevitably fail. Nonetheless, it did suggest that any such experiment should be approached with great caution.

KW: Prisons / Private / United States

100 Maeir, D. M. 1978. "The Impossibility of 'Informed Consent'." Pp. 17-27 in *Medical Experimentation*, edited by A. Carmi. Ramat-Gan, Israel: Turtledove Publishing.

Presents the issue of informed consent in relation to experimentation using solicited individuals who are studied, not for their benefit, but for the gain of valuable scientific knowledge and perhaps "for other patients" in general without harm or risk to the subjects.

KW: Informed consent / Prisoners

101 Nachshon, I. and M. Rotenberg. 1977. "Perception of Violence By Institutionalized Offenders." *Journal of Criminal Law and Criminology* 68:454-7.

Examines whether ambiguous stimuli were perceived differently by criminals and non criminals. Reports that criminals perceived ambiguous stimuli as violent while non-criminals perceived them as having non-violent content.

KW: Juvenile delinquency / Prisoners / Violence

102 Shapira, R. and D. Navon. 1986. "Cooperation Between Inmates and Staff in Israeli Prisons: Towards a Non-Functionalist Theory of Total Institutions." Pp. 181-202 in *People in Institutions: The Israeli Scene,* edited by Y. Kashti and M. Arieli. London: Freund Publishing House.

Examines the nature of Israeli prisons for interpersonal relations based on Goffman's theory of total institutions. The authors identify prisons as total institutions in four ways: boundary breakage, adjustment of individual to group, dictation of all activities, and channeling of activities to achieve institutional objectives.

KW: Interpersonal relations / Prison guards / Prisoners / Prisons / Total institutions

103 Shavitt, G. 1976. "Prison Labor and Its Wages: A Review and Proposal." *Israel Studies in Criminology* III:24-54.

KW: Employment / Prisoners / Vocational training / Wages

104 Shichor, D. 1976. "Some Impacts of a New Correctional Policy on Organizational Rules and Sanctioning." *Israel Studies in Criminology* III:55-71.

KW: Correctional policy / Treatment methods

105 Shichor, D. 1979. "Decision-Making in Institutional Settings." *Residential & Community Child Care Administration* 1(2):121-40.

Provides a brief review of the literature pertaining to participation in the decision-making process of organizational members and the possible connections between this participation and the achievement of organizational goals. The focus of the discussion is the juvenile correctional setting.

KW: Decision Making / Residential setting

106 Shichor, D. 1987. "Penal Policies: Some Recent Trends." *Legal Studies Forum* XI(1):55-78.

Provides a brief review of the sources of criticism against rehabilitation on the theoretical level, and the resulting policies which replaced treatment as the major method of handling offenders. Offers observations regarding future trends in penology including the projected revival of the rehabilitation ideal.

KW: Penology / Policy

107 Shichor, D. 1992. "Myths and Realities in Prison Siting." *Crime & Delinquency* 38(1):70-87.

Reviews the arguments for and against the siting of a correctional facility in a community. Arguments for siting were usually based on the economic benefits for the community. However, the appeal of these benefits varied with different communities and among various groups. Opposition resulted from many reasons such as fear of escapes, decline in property values, prisoners' families, quality of life concerns, and feelings of inefficacy. Future sitings would likely be in economically depressed communities where economic benefits of the siting make the most difference.

KW: Prisons

108 Shichor, D. and H. E. Allen. 1977. "Study Release: A Correctional Alternative." *Offender Rehabilitation* 2(1):7-17.

The authors describe a study release program which attempted to bring the inmate back into the community by providing educational skills that are important and highly valued in achievement-oriented modern societies.

They recommend that research be conducted to evaluate such programs.

KW: Correctional rehabilitation / Study release

109 Shichor, D. and L. T. Empey. 1974. "A Typological Analysis of Correctional Organizations." *Sociology and Social Research* 58(3):318-34.

An organizational typology was constructed to expand the knowledge of existing organizations and act as a rudimentary theoretical framework by which alternative structures might be developed. According to this typology, correctional organizations are characterized by goal orientation (custodial/treatment), scope of interaction (internal/external) and the nature of decision making (preemptory/participatory).

KW: Juvenile delinquency / Residential institutions / Typology / Youth rehabilitation

110 Shmulevitz, H. 1990. "Imprisonment: The Israeli Perspective." Pp. 87-93 in *The Prevention of Crime and the Treatment of Offenders in Israel*, edited by Y. Tzubery, A Report to the Eighth UN Congress on the Prevention of Crime and the Treatment of Offenders, Havana, August 27 to September 7. Jerusalem: Ministry of Police.

This description of the Israeli prison service system details the procedure of intake, diagnosis and classification of new inmates, treatment of inmates, inmate petitions, and administrative release.

KW: Prisoners / Prisons

111 Shoham, S. G. 1989. "Personality Correlates of Violent Prisoners." *Personality and Individual Differences* 10(2):137-45.

Assesses a learning module to teach high school students inquiry skills.

KW: Personality traits / Prisoners / Violence

112 Shoham, S. G. 1989. "Social Attitude Correlates of Violent Prisoners." *Personality and Individual Differences* 10(2):147-53.

KW: Prisoners / Social attitudes / Violence

113 Shoham, S. G., J. J. M. Askenasy, G. Rahav, F. Chard and A. Addi. 1988. "Personality and Social Attitude of Violent Prisoners." *Medicine and Law* 7:269-86.

See article on "Violent Prisoners," pp. 247-67 in the same issue (also see entry #115). This article emphasizes the sociological aspects of violent prisoners.

KW: Personality traits / Prisoners / Social attitudes / Violence

114 Shoham, S. G., J. J. M. Askenasy, G. Rahav, F. Chard and A. Addi. 1989. "Some Biological Predispositions and Multivariate Analysis of the Bio-Psycho-Social Correlates of Violent Prisoners." *Medicine and Law* 7:607-28.

This is a test of a hypothetical multi-dimensional model to identify violent prisoners. Sensory stimuli were absorbed by the nervous system and created nervous reaction (endocrinological responses). These reactions were interpreted by personality parameters structured along socio-cultural patterns.

KW: Behavior disorders / Models / Nervous system disorders / Personality traits / Prisoners / Psychophysiology / Sociobiology / Violence

115 Shoham, S. G., J. J. M. Askenasy, G. Rahav, F. Chard, A. Addi and M. Addad. 1988. "Violent Prisoners." *Medicine and Law* 7:247-67.

Presents an interdisciplinary model for the study of violence and incorporates a hierarchy of levels of etiology: biological potential, personality structuring and social imprints. Also contains an updated review of the literature. The model synchronizes electro-encephalographical data, endocrinological data, Shoham's personality theory, family dynamics and societal attitudes towards law enforcement.

KW: Literature review / Prisoners / Violence

116 Shoham, S. G., G. Rahav, R. Markowski, F. Chard, F. Neuman, M. Ben-Haim, I. Baruch, Y. Esformes, Z. Schwarzman, R. Rubin, S. Mednick and W. Buickhuisen. 1987. "Family Parameters of Violent Prisoners." *The Journal of Social Psychology* 127(1):83-91.

This is an interdisciplinary study of violence that focuses on the subjects' family relations. Most violent offenders were found to be from North Africa, characterized by planned behavior. A relationship was found between "problematic family" and violence (a similar relationship was not found for non-violent crime).

KW: Ethnic origin / Family relations / Personality traits / Prisoners / Violence

117 Shoham, S. and G. Rahav and E. Segal. 1973. "The Classification of Prisoners in Israel." *Abstracts on Criminology and Penology* 13(3):257-63.

KW: Behavior patterns / Classification / Models / Prisoners

118 Shoham, S., E. Segal and G. Rahav. 1973. "The Classification of Prisoners in Israel." *Israel Studies in Criminology* III:13-23.

This is an attempted to test Clinard and Quinney's model for criminal behavior systems. The study found that the model was not applicable (without modifications) to Israel for career criminals.

KW: Behavior patterns / Classification / Crime / Models / Prisoners

119 Sigal, M., I. Carmel, D. Altmark and P. Silfen. 1988. "Munchausen Syndrome by Proxy: A Psychodynamic Analysis." *Medicine and Law* 7:49-56.

The authors treated this syndrome as one that is expressed in husband-wife relations and other symbiotic relations. Explain the psychopathological and psychodynamic background for the syndrome's development and maintain that the source of the problem was in the ability to establish relations during early childhood.

KW: Interpersonal relations / Mental disorders

120 Silfen, P. 1977. "The Adaptation of Older Prisoners in Israel." *International Journal of Offender Therapy and Comparative Criminology* 21(1):57-65.
Describes perceptions of prisoners about aging, future plans, self-esteem, relationships with others and dependence on peers or guards.

KW: Adjustment / Aging / Prisoners

121 Silfen, P., S. Ben-David, D. Kliger, and R. Eshel. 1978. "Preparedness of Israeli Prisoners to Participate in Medical Experiments." Pp. 59-78 in *Medical Experimentation*, edited by A. Carmi. Ramat-Gan, Israel: Turtledove Publishing.
Examines the extent to which prisoners were prepared to participate in medical experiments, including new medications, mental health therapy and drug withdrawal. Found that in Israel, unlike in most countries (including the United States) prisoners were least prepared to participate in experiments on new medications.

KW: Medical experiments / Prisoners

122 Wolins, M. and Y. Wozner. 1977. "Deinstitutionalization and the Benevolent Asylum." *Social Service Review* 51(4):604-23.
Discusses the influence of community-based rehabilitation trends on deviants. Argued that through the human deinstitutionalization of some, others were left behind as a "cursed community."

KW: Deinstitutionalization / Disabilities / Organizational change / Rehabilitation / Residential institutions

123 Wolins, M. and Y. Wozner. 1982. *Revitalizing Residential Settings*. San Francisco: Jossey-Bass.
Provides an in-depth analysis of residential settings, operational aspects, goals and factors contributing to the success/failure of the institution. Discusses the attitudes and perceptions of care providers and service recipients as to settings' expectations.

KW: Boarding schools / Interpersonal relations / Residential institutions

124 Wozner, Y. 1979. "Positive Control in Institutions." *Residential & Community Child Care Administration* 1(2):187-205.

KW: Rewards / Social control / Total institutions

125 Wozner, Y. 1982. "Assessing the Quality of Internat Life." *Human Relations* 35(11):1059-72.

Divides treatment institutions into two types: Rehabilitative - those that seek to change the patient and improve a situation, and non-rehabilitative - that is not interested in the patient's welfare. Offers an instrument to define institutional environment based on the Quality of Life Map.

KW: Environment / Personality change / Quality of life / Rehabilitation / Total institutions

126 Wozner, Y. 1986. "The Intensive Educational Internat." Pp. 107-35 in *People in Institutions: The Israeli Scene,* edited by Y. Kashti and M. Arieli. London: Freund Publishing House.

Presents a model of an intensive education boarding school geared towards youth who dropped out from all educational environments. Pupils indicated an increase in self-esteem and in motivation for self-rehabilitation.

KW: Behavioral change / Boarding schools / Self-concept / Student behavior / Youth in distress / Youth rehabilitation

127 Wozner, Y. 1987. "Social Work in Internats." Pp. 267-82 in *Residential Settings and the Community: Congruence and Conflict*, edited by Y. Kashti and M. Arieli. London: Freund.

Discusses social work's role in residential treatment. Also describes residential sub-systems, objectives and functions of the residential social worker and time allocation.

KW: Job descriptions / Residential institutions / Social work

128 Wozner, Y. 1991. "People Care in Institutions: A Conceptual Schema and Its Application." *Child and Youth Care Services* 15(1):1-237.

Analyzed operational principles and strategies of institutions that treat persons out of their homes (such as hospitals, nursing homes, prisons, military boot camps, monasteries). These were called internats and were on a continuum of autocratic and total organization. In a rewarding system the elements of motivation, participation and attention need to be found.

KW: Evaluation / Intervention programs / Organizational climate / Organizational structure / Quality of life / Residential institutions

129 Wozner, Y. 1991. "Program Integration in Residential Care: The Residential Center as the Instrument of Care Delivery." Pp. 255-72 in *The Child and Youth Care Worker in Residential Setting: Knowledge Utilization in Direct Care Practice*, edited by J. Beker and Z. Eisikovits. New York, Child Welfare League of America, Inc.

This chapter presents some organizational considerations with regard to the services offered by internats that are important for direct child and youth care workers as well as administrators and other professionals who work in such settings.

KW: Residential institutions

130 Yinon, Y., and I. Tannenbaum. 1974. "Employers' Attitudes Towards the Employment of Ex-Convicts in Israel." Pp. 41-54 in *Victimology: A New focus, Vol. II, Society's Reaction to Victimization*, edited by I. Drapkin and E. Viano. Lexington, MA: Lexington Books.

KW: Attitudes / Employers / Personnel selection / Prisoners

3

Correctional Treatment

131 Ben-David, S. 1992. "Influence, Leadership and Social Desirability in Psychotherapeutic Groups." *Journal of Group Psychotherapy, Psychodrama, and Sociometry* 45(1):17-23.

Examines leadership in psychotherapeutic groups and the correlation between social desirability and influence in the group. Three leader types were found: The popular, acceptable and influential (among sex offenders), unpopular yet influential (violent robbers), and the sociometric star was found in all other groups irrespective of his influence level.

KW: Crime / Group work / Leadership / Prisoners / Psychotherapy / Social acceptance / Sociometry

132 Cohen, B-Z. 1985. "A Cognitive Approach to the Treatment of Offenders." *British Journal of Social Work* 15:619-33.

Attempted to apply the principles of cognitive therapy to treat adult offenders. Discusses the applicability of cognitive therapy to criminal behavior.

KW: Cognitive therapy / Crime / Offenders

133 Cohen, B-Z. 1988. "Reality Therapy in Probation and Correctional Counseling." *Issues in Correctional Training and Casework* 4:24-8.

Discusses the principles of reality therapy and its use in counseling and probation services for criminals. This theory is based on five principles: involvement, present behavior, behavior assessment, negotiation, and commitment.

KW: Behavioral change / Counseling services / Crime / Probation / Reality therapy / Treatment methods

134 Cohen, B-Z. and I. Sordo. 1984. "Using Reality Therapy with Adult Offenders." *Journal of Offender Counseling, Services & Rehabilitation* 8(3):25-39.

This study claims to present a corrected version of reality therapy as used with adult offenders. It argues that reality therapy could, in fact, offer a way for more responsible behavior for most adult offenders.

KW: Adults / Crime / Reality therapy

135 Dauber, E. and D. Shichor. 1979. "A Comparative Exploration of Prison Discipline." *Journal of Criminal Justice* 7:21-36.

Explores the formal disciplinary procedures of the Ramle prison in Israel in comparison to the Rhode Island prison. Generally it was found that the disciplinary process in Ramle was more flexible and relaxed than the similar process in Rhode Island. Compares and reviews the possible advantages and disadvantages of the two systems.

KW: Discipline / Prisons

136 Erez, E. 1987. "Rehabilitation in Justice: The Prisoner's Perspective." *Journal of Offender Counseling, Services & Rehabilitation* 11(2):5-19.

KW: Correctional rehabilitation

137 Erez, E. 1988. "Ethical and Legal Issues in Program Evaluation." Pp. 167-99 in *Evaluation Research and Decision Guidance: Correctional, Addiction-Treatment, Mental Health and Other People Changing Agencies*, edited by D. Glaser with E. Erez, New Brunswick, NJ: Transaction Books.

KW: Ethics / Program evaluation

138 Fisher, M., M. Teichman, and B. Geiger. 1985. "The Rehabilitation of Young Israeli Offenders: A Kibbutz Experiment." *International Journal of Offender Therapy and Comparative Criminology* 29(3):277-80.

Describes a kibbutz-based rehabilitation program that started in January 1983. The program is based on group dynamics and social learning theory and took place on kibbutz premises within a non-compulsory atmosphere.

KW: Correctional rehabilitation / Intervention programs / Juvenile delinquency / Kibbutzim

139 Glaser, D. with E. Erez. 1988. *Evaluation Research and Decision Guidance: Correctional, Addiction-Treatment, Mental Health and Other People Changing Agencies*, edited by D. Glaser with E. Erez, New Brunswick, NJ: Transaction Books.

KW: Evaluation research / People changing agencies / Program evaluation

140 Gottlieb, A. 1986. "Rehabilitating Disattached Youths in Residential Centers: Problems and Prospects." Pp. 37-64 in *People in Institutions: The Israeli Scene,* edited by Y. Kashti and M. Arieli. London: Freund Publishing House.

Describes "Manoff," a residential institution in northern Israel that houses youth who dropped out from all school or occupational settings. Admission criteria are discussed along with various activity plans, staff, youth behavior and achievement.

KW: Boarding schools / Evaluation research / Intervention programs /

Juvenile delinquency / Rehabilitation / Youth in distress

141 Hermon, Z. 1965. "The Institutional Treatment and After-Care of Adult Offenders and Juvenile Delinquents in Israel." Pp. 122-64 in *The Prevention of Crime and the Treatment of Offenders in Israel*, A Report to the Third UN Congress on the Prevention of Crime and the Treatment of Offenders, Stockholm, August 9 to 18, Jerusalem, Israel: Government Printer.

KW: After-care / Correctional rehabilitation / Juvenile delinquency / Prisoners

142 Kashti, Y. and M. Arieli. 1986. *People in Institutions: The Israeli Scene*. London: Freund Publishing House.
This book constitutes a collection of empirical and theoretical articles on what the authors call the "ethos and social realities in Israeli institutions."

KW: Child welfare / Children / Residential settings

143 Kashti, Y., M. Arieli, and Y. Wozner. 1981. "The Israeli Residential Setting: Tradition, Social Context, Organization." Pp. 1-81 in *Residential Education in Israel*, edited by R. Shapira and C. Adler. Jerusalem, June.

KW: Boarding schools

144 Munin, M. and A. Jarus. 1970. "Residential Treatment Services for Emotionally Disturbed Children in Israel." Pp. 519-40 in *Children and Families in Israel: Some Mental Health Perspectives*, edited by A. Jarus, J. Marcus, J. Oren and C. Rapaport, London: Gordon and Breach.

KW: Emotional disturbance / Mental health / Residential services / Treatment

145 Rahav, G. 1980. "TM and Rehabilitation: Another View." *Criminal Justice and Behavior* 7:11-7.

KW: Rehabilitation

146 Scott, J. E., S. Dinitz and D. Shichor. 1978. "Pioneering Innovations in Corrections: Shock Probation and Shock Parole." *Offender Rehabilitation* 3(2):113-22.
This article provides a brief description of these two innovative methods of correction. A theoretical analysis, based on the principles of punishment, and an empirical review pointed out their possible contributions to contemporary corrections. They seem to have reduced incarceration and shortened the length of imprisonment.

KW: Innovations / Parole / Probation

147 Shichor, D. 1992. "Following the Penological Pendulum: The Survival of Rehabilitation." *Federal Probation* 56(2):19-25.

Reviews the penological developments of the last two decades. Indicate that a major change occurred in punishment ideology and control measures from rehabilitative orientation to "neo-retributive" orientation on the one hand and to "neo-utilitarian" orientation on the other.

KW: Penology / Rehabilitation

148 Shoham, S. G. 1986. "The Existentialist Approach to Penal and Mental Treatment." *Israel Studies in Criminology* VII:157-71.

Presents the relevance of utilizing an existential approach to treat criminals. This approach attempts to change the person's internal environment when the external environment cannot be changed. Offers implementation steps for prison environment.

KW: Correctional rehabilitation / Educational philosophy / Personality change / Treatment methods

149 Shoham, S. and Z. Slonim. 1963. "The Moral Dilemma of Penal Treatment." *The Juridical Review: The Law Journal of the Scottish Universities*, Scotland, August, p. 185

Discusses the role of the "treatment man" and the challenges of making law abiding citizens out of criminals. The dilemma was that the knowledge base to meet this challenge was insufficient for him to be effective.

KW: Moral dilemma / Prisons / Treatment

150 Silfen, P. 1985. "Prison-Psychiatry: Medical or Correctional Discipline?" *Medicine and Law* 4: 239-49.

Summarizes different aspects of health services in prisons focusing particularly on mental health. Deals with ethical, clinical, and organizational problems in prison mental health.

KW: Health services / Literature review / Mental health / Prisons / Psychiatry

151 Silfen, P. 1986. "Psychotherapy of Mentally Disturbed Criminals: Illusion or Reality?" *Medicine and Law* 5:427-31.

With the change in treatment policies, emphasis was given to treatment in the broadest sense of the term. Argues that the mental pathology of offenders has changed and with it the need to reexamine new methods and goals for treatment.

KW: Mental disorders / Prisons / Psychotherapy

152 Silfen, P. and C. Hechal. 1986. "Therapeutic Work with Drug Addicts in Prison." *Medicine and Law* 5:505-13.

Describes an experimental treatment of drug addicts within prison based on the psychoanalytic approach. Success was reported in shifting from relationship with the drug to relationships with others.

KW: Drug addiction / Drug rehabilitation / Prisoners / Psychotherapy / Prisons / Mental disorders

153 Tzubery, Y., ed. 1990. *The Prevention of Crime and the Treatment of Offenders in Israel*, A Report to the Eighth UN Congress on the Prevention of Crime and the Treatment of Offenders, Havana, August 27 to September 7. Jerusalem: Ministry of Police.

A collection of articles on crime prevention and treatment of offenders in Israel. Reviews major prevention methods, international cooperation and examined the Israeli approach to prison alternatives and rehabilitation.

KW: Crime / Crime prevention / Imprisonment alternatives / Rehabilitation

154 Weiner, A. 1986. "Pre-School Residential Care: The Case of Neve Taf." Pp. 83-92 /in *People in Institutions: The Israeli Scene,* edited by Y. Kashti and M. Arieli. London: Freund Publishing House.

Examines the awareness of Israeli institutions to the dangers embedded in institutions for children at very young age. Offers program components that might reduce the negative impact institutions may have on the child.

KW: Boarding schools / Case study / Early childhood / Residential institutions

155 Williams, F. P., D. Shichor and A. H. Wiggenhorn. 1989. "Fine Tuning Social Control: Electronic Monitoring and Surrogate Homes for Drug Using Parolees. A Research Note." *Journal of Contemporary Criminal Justice* 5(3):173-80.

Initial results from the program suggested that the combination of electronic monitoring and surrogate homes may even be effective for drug-using parole violators.

KW: Electronic monitoring / Parole / Social control / Surrogate homes

156 Wolins, M., Y. Wozner and S. Shye. 1980. "Rejuvenating the Asylum: A Field Study." *Social Work Research and Abstracts* 16(1):17-25.

Examines whether there was a relationship between information flow and improvement in the functioning of the boarding facility. Workers saw a direct relationship, but it was more moderate among the boarders.

KW: Asylum / Boarding schools / Information transfer / Juvenile delinquency

157 Wozner, Y. 1979. "Positive Control in Institutions." *Residential & Community Child Care Administration* 1(2):187-205.

This article perceives of institutional treatment as controlling the patients and staff alike. Humanization of treatment could be achieved through reduction of the "totality" of control by increasing activities within, increasing involvement of staff and increasing interaction with the community.

KW: Involvement / Rewards / Social control / Total institutions

158 Wozner, Y. 1981. "The Internat - The Residential Setting for Treatment of Specialized Populations." Pp. 138-42 in *Residential Education in Israel*, Report of the Israeli-American Seminar on Out of School Education, edited by R. Shapira and C. Adler. Jerusalem: Ministry of Education and Culture, June.

KW: Residential institutions

159 Wozner, Y. 1985. "Institution as Community." *Child and Youth Care Services* 7(3-4):71-89.
The article presents the seven basic ideas for a community: status, role definition, mobility, unity, punishment, communication and decision making. Unity of value system is argued to be the most important variable.

KW: Institutions / Organizational structure / Youth villages

4

Crime and Society

160 Amir, M. and R. Simon. 1990. "Legal Statutes and Public Attitudes Toward Censorship and Freedom of Expression in Israel." *Studies in Communications* 4:39-48.

KW: Censorship / Freedom of expression / Public opinion

161 Bensinger, G. J. 1981. "Old Habits Die Hard: 'Vengeance is Ours,' Saith Israel's Arab Community." *Law Enforcement News* VII(17):12.

Discusses the cultural norms and patterns of Israeli Arabs in resolving disputes by juxtaposing "Arab justice" with "Israeli justice." Also mentions retributive killings and the concept of vengeance and reconciliation.

KW: Arabs in Israel / Disputes

162 Bensinger, G. J. 1992. "Hate Crimes: A New/Old Problem." *International Journal of Comparative and Applied Criminal Justice* 16(1):115-23

Reviews and assesses some of the more recent developments and policies concerning hate crimes in different jurisdictions and concluded that despite the new efforts underway, hate crimes represent a challenge to law enforcement that still needs to be met.

KW: Hate crimes

163 Chen, M. and C. Pincus. 1973. "The Stranger in the Classroom Society." *Israel Studies in Criminology* II:103-12.

KW: Alienation / Immigrants / Social acceptance / Social adjustment / Students

164 Cohen, S. 1989. *Crime, Justice and Social Control in the Israeli Arab Population.* Tel-Aviv: International Centre for Peace in the Middle East.

KW: Arabs in Israel / Crime / Social control

165 Cohen, S. 1990. "Politics and Crime in Israel: Reactions from the Home Front." *Social Justice* 17(1):5-13

A collection of reactions the author published in the first two years of the Intifada (Arab uprising in occupied territories). The reactions reflected, according to the author, the limits of the intellectual world in dealing with a difficult reality.

KW: Crime / Criminology / Intellectuals / Intifada (uprising) / Politics / Social systems

166 Deutsch, J., S. Hakim and J. Weinblatt. 1984. "Interjurisdictional Criminal Mobility: A Theoretical Perspective." *Urban Studies* 21(4):451-8.

KW: Crime / Criminological theories / Criminal mobility

167 Drapkin, I. 1989. *Crime and Punishment in the Ancient World.* Lexington, MA: Lexington Books.

The book has two parts. The first part includes chapters on the legacy of primitive man, ancient civilizations in Mesopotamia, Pharaonic Egypt, ancient Hebrew criminal law, law of the Medes and Persians, ancient India and the laws of the Manu, imperial China, ancient and classical Greece, and Roman criminal law. The second part includes the laws of the Shari'a (Islam), Fetha Nagast (Ethiopia), the Basques, early and feudal Japan, and Oceanea.

KW: Comparative research / Crime / Historical research / Punishment

168 Erez, E. 1980. "Planning of Crime and the Criminal Career: Official and Hidden Offenses." *Journal of Criminal Law and Criminology* 71(1):73-6.

KW: Crime / Crime planning / Criminal careers / Hidden statistics / Official statistics

169 Erez, E. 1984. "On the 'Dark Figure' of Arrest." *Journal of Police Science and Administration* 12(4):431-40.

This research note examines the ambiguity associated with the term "arrest," its multiplicity of meanings in the criminal justice area, and the correspondence between various measures or operational definitions of arrest.

KW: Arrest / Crime / Dark figure of arrest

170 Erez, E. 1988. "The Myth of the New Female Offender: Some Evidence from Attitudes Toward Law and Justice." *Journal of Criminal Justice* 16(6):499-509.

KW: Attitudes / Crime / Female offender / Women

171 Erez, E. and E. Appelbaum. 1984. "The Effects of Precision of Sentencing Information on Crime Rates: A Theoretical Model." *Journal of Criminal Justice* 12(5):503-8.

KW: Crime / Crime rates / Models / Sentencing

172 Erez, E. and S. Hakim. 1979. "A Geo-Economic Approach to the Distribution of Crime in Metropolitan Areas." Pp. 29-47 in *Perspectives on Victimology*, edited by W. Parsonage, Beverly Hills, CA: Sage.

KW: Crime / Urban areas

173 Figlio, R. M., S. Hakim and G. F. Rengert, eds. 1986. *Metropolitan Crime Patterns*. Monsey, NY: Criminal Justice Press.

KW: Crime / Urban areas

174 Fishman, G. and S. Dinitz. 1989. "Japan: A Country with Safe Streets." *Advances in Criminological Theory* 1:111-26, edited by W. S. Laufer and F. Adler, New Brunswick, NJ: Transaction Publishers.

KW: Criminological theories / Japan / Public safety

175 Fishman, G., V. Kraus and B-Z. Cohen. 1986. "A Multidimensional Approach to the Problem of Crime Seriousness." *International Journal of Comparative and Applied Criminal Justice* 10(2):177-91.

Examines a new approach to cope with methodological and theoretical problems criminologists face. The least serious offenses were economic and white collar crimes while homicide was the most serious and so was rape. Offenses were ranked according to intent and damage.

KW: Crime seriousness / Homicide / Social attitudes

176 Ginat, J. 1979. "Illicit Sexual Relationships and Family Honor in Arab Society." *Israel Studies in Criminology* V:179-204.

Examines normative behavior with regards to illicit sexual behavior and found that murder against that backdrop took place only when there was a public accusation of the aggrieved party, typically accompanied by personal or political motives.

KW: Arabs in Israel / Bedouins / Murder / Sexual behavior / Social norms

177 Ginat, J. 1986. "The Role of the Mediator: With Special Reference to Blood Disputes." *Israel Studies in Criminology* VII:98-131.

This is an anthropological discussion of the "mediator's" role in settling blood disputes (feuds) in different cultures. It argues that mediators used their authority by activating their special connections in the community and with the legal authorities.

KW: Bedouins / Homicide

178 Hakim, S. 1980. "The Attraction of Property Crimes to Suburban Localities: A Revised Economic Model." *Urban Studies* 17(3):265-76.

KW: Economic model / Property crimes / Suburbs / Thefts

179 Hassin, Y. and M. Amir. 1976. "'Business (Crime) as Usual' in Wartime Conditions Among Offenders in Israel." *Journal of Criminal Law and Criminology* 66(4):491-5.

Compares crime patterns in Israel during the Yom-Kippur war (1973) and peacetime criminality. The first week of war evidenced a sharp decrease but after that crime returned to its usual level.

KW: Comparative research / Crime / War influences / Yom-Kippur War

180 O'Brien, R. M., D. Shichor and D. L. Decker. 1980. "An Empirical Comparison of the Validity of UCR and NCS Crime Rates." *The Sociological Quarterly* 21(3):391-401.

Assesses the validity of these two indicators of crime rates for six different types of crimes, by examining their "convergent" and "nomological" validity. Results are discussed in light of this comparison.

KW: Crime / Empirical comparison / NCS crime rates / UCR crime rates

181 Rahav, G. and L. Ellis. 1990. "International Crime Rates and Evolutionary Theory: An Application of the r/K Selection Concept to Human Populations." Pp. 115-20 in *Crime in Biological, Social, and Moral Contexts*, edited by L. Ellis and H. Hoffman. New York: Praeger.

This is a preliminary test of the r/K selection-criminality hypothesis (groups who are more prone towards criminality should be less K-selected than those who are less prone) at an international level. It sought to determine whether societies with the highest crime rates exhibit r-selected characteristics to a greater extent than populations with the lower crime rates.

KW: Crime / Evolutionary theory / International crime rates

182 Rahav G. and S. Jaamdar. 1982. "Development and Crime: A Cross National Study." *Development and Change* 13:447-62.

KW: Crime / Cross national study

183 Raveh, A. and S. F. Landau. 1986. "Smallest Space Analysis vs. The Method of Principal Components: Another Look at Ahamad's Analysis of Crimes." *Journal of Quantitative Criminology* 2(3):279-91.

This study is a re-analysis the Ahamad case study of 18 types of offenses. The suggested method was a nonmetric multidimensional scaling type called Smallest Space Analysis (SSA-I) which uncovered findings that were not expressed explicitly by the principal-components method used by Ahamad.

KW: Crime / Juvenile delinquency / Smallest Space Analysis / Statistical methodology

184 Schmelz, U. O. 1969. "Differentials in Criminality Rates between Various Groups in Israel's Population." Pp. 264-319 in *Scripta Hierosolymitana*, Vol. 21, *Studies in Criminology*, edited by I. Drapkin. Jerusalem: The Magnes Press, The Hebrew University.

KW: Crime / Crime rates

185 Shichor, D. 1985. "Effects of Development on Official Crime Rates, 1967-1978: Homicide and Larceny Patterns Differ Greatly." *Sociology and Social Research* 70(1):96-7.

Following Preben Wolf's analysis this study focuses on crime and economic conditions and found similar patterns to other studies indicating that modernization usually brought with it more larceny and somewhat less homicide.

KW: Crime / Development / Homicide / Larceny

186 Shichor, D. 1990. "Crime Patterns and Socioeconomic Development: A Cross-National Analysis." *Criminal Justice Review* 15(1):64-78.

Explores the relationship between the rates and patterns of crime and various socioeconomic factors. Using Interpol crime data and socioeconomic statistics of 44 countries, multivariate analysis was conducted for three periods. Modernization did not have a uniform effect and over time the predictive powers concerning crime may change.

KW: Comparative research / Crime / Development / Modernization / Socioeconomic variables

187 Shichor, D. and J. W. Heeren. 1989. "Social Control in Socialist Societies: An Analysis of Five Major Characteristics." *Legal Studies Forum* 13(3):215-38.

This study argues that analysis of formal social control that follows the Marxist-socialist ideology focuses on community care. Formal controls identified were adaptation of the crime control model, politicization of offenses, rehabilitation-reeducation of offenders, pervasiveness of control and encouragement of mass participation.

KW: Social control / Socialism

188 Shinnar, S. and R. Shinnar. 1975. "The Effects of the Criminal Justice System on the Control of Crime: A Quantitative Approach." *Law & Society Review* 9(4):581-611.

Attempts to elaborate on a recent paper where one of the authors developed a mathematical model simple enough to make approximate quantitative estimates of crime and its prevention. In this article the model is simplified even further in a way that will make it more accessible to the policy maker and social scientist.

KW: Crime / Crime control / Criminal law

189 Shoham, S. 1966. "Criminology in Israel." *The Juridical Review: The Law Journal of the Scottish Universities*, Scotland.

This article suggests that the larger the conflict between legal norms, social norms and societal values, the larger the crime rate. It examines different ethnic groups in Israel and the influence of different immigrations on the crime rate in general and on juvenile delinquency in particular. Crime is viewed as a result of conflicting values and cultures among new immigrants.

KW: Crime / Crime causes / Criminal law / Cultural differences / Ethnic origin / Juvenile delinquency / New immigrants / Social norms

190 Shoham, S. and G. Rahav. 1968. *The Measurement of Movements on the Conformity-Deviance Continuum as an Auxiliary Tool for Action Research.* Jerusalem: Ministry of Education and Culture, Youth Development Research Unit in Collaboration with the Department of Psychology, University of Tel-Aviv. Also published as Shoham, S. G., G. Rahav and A. Kreisler. 1970. "The Measurement of Movements on the Conformity-Deviance Continuum as an Auxiliary Tool for Action Research." *Acta Criminologica* III:103-42.

KW: Action research / Conformity / Deviance / Measurement

191 Simon, R. J. 1977. "Women and Crime in Israel." Pp. 81-90 in *Criminology in Perspective: Essays in Honors of Israel Drapkin*, edited by S. F. Landau and L. Sebba. Lexington, MA: Lexington Books.

Assuming that women's liberation should be reflected in increase in the extent and scope of crime among women, it was found that while this assumption was born out in the U.S. and England, this was not the case in Israel.

KW: Crime / Comparative research / Secondary data analysis / United Kingdom / United States / Women

192 Simon, R. J., J. M. Landis and M. Amir. 1989. "Jewish and Arab Perceptions of Civil Rights in Israel." *Studies in Law, Politics and Society* 10:245-62.

KW: Arabs in Israel / Civil rights / Jews / Social perception

193 Weimann, G. and G. Fishman. 1988. "Attribution of Responsibility: Sex-Based Bias in Press Reports on Crime." *European Journal of Communication* 3:415-30.

Examines the "chivalry hypothesis" as related to media portrayals of female criminality. Attribution of responsibility statements were classified by type of offense, offender's sex and other variables. Interaction between the offender's sex and the type of crime influenced the tendency of the press to present the offender as a "pawn" or as an "origin" type criminal.

KW: Content analysis / Crime / Media / Sex stereotypes / Women

5

Crime by and among the Aged

194 Amir, M. 1989. "Aging in Organized Crime." Pp. 61-85 in *Older Offenders: Current Trends*, edited by C. Burnett and S. Chaneles. Haworth Press. Also published as "Aging and Aged in Organized Crime." *Journal of Offender Counseling, Services & Rehabilitation* 13(2):61-85.

Discusses the relationship between organized crime and old age following arrests in Italy and the U.S. of criminals 68-72 old. Findings indicated that elderly were active, potent and independent and continued to manage and lead organized crime.

KW: Aged / Aging / Italy / Organized crime / United States

195 Amir, M. and S. Bergman. 1976. "Patterns of Crime among the Aged in Israel: Second Phase Report." *Israel Annals of Psychiatry and Related Disciplines* 14(3):280-8.

This study found that characteristics of crimes by the aged in Israel showed no difference from adult population on gender, origin, immigration and socioeconomic status but were unique in terms of types of crimes, recidivism and sentencing.

KW: Aged / Crime

196 Bergman, S. and M. Amir. 1973. "Crime and Delinquency among Aged in Israel: An Experience Survey." *Israel Annals of Psychiatry and Related Disciplines* 11(1):33-48.

This is an attempt to fill the knowledge gap about old age criminality. Offers a review of the literature, analysis of the elderly criminal population, and reports the results of a survey on attitudes, opinions, policy, trends and scope of the problem as seen by a cross-section of the professional community.

KW: Aged / Crime / Survey

197 Bergman, S. and M. Amir. 1973. "Crime and Delinquency among the Aged in Israel" *Geriatrics* 28(1):149-57.

KW: Aged / Crime

198 Shichor, D. 1984. "The Extent and Nature of Lawbreaking by the Elderly: A Review of Arrest Statistics." Pp. 17-32 in *Elderly Criminals*, edited by E. S. Newman, D. J. Newman and M. L. Gewirtz. Cambridge, MA: Oelgeschlager, Gunn and Hain.

Reviews official statistics finding out that in relative terms arrests among the elderly constituted only a small part of the total arrests.

KW: Crime / Elderly / Statistics

199 Shichor, D. 1984. "Patterns of Elderly Lawbreaking in Urban, Suburban, and Rural Areas: What Do Arrest Statistics Tell Us?" Pp. 53-63 in *Elderly Criminals*, edited by W. Wilbanks and P. K. H. Kim. Washington, DC: University Press of America.

The general trend indicated, as expected, that the large majority of elderly arrests occurred in cities. However, over the 16-year time period covered by the study, the share of suburban arrests of the total elderly arrests has increased substantially while the relative share of the city arrests was on the decline.

KW: Crime / Elderly / Statistics

200 Shichor, D. 1985. "Male-Female Difference in Elderly Arrests: An Exploratory Analysis." *Justice Quarterly* 2(3):399-414.

This study analyzed arrest statistics revealing that there were more differences in arrests between elderly males and females than between males and females in the general population. The issue of differential handling of females and the elderly by law enforcement agencies could not be dealt with sufficiently using these statistics, although it could be inferred from some arrest patterns that elderly females might have been handled more leniently than others where minor offenses were concerned.

KW: Crime / Elderly / Gender differences

201 Shichor, D. 1988. "An Exploratory Study of Elderly Probationers." *International Journal of Offender Therapy and Comparative Criminology* 32(23):163-74.

Focuses on elderly offenders' probation, their characteristics, issues connected with their handling by the criminal justice system in general, and the probation in particular.

KW: Crime / Elderly / Probation

202 Shichor, D. and S. Bergman. 1979. "Patterns of Suicide among Elderly in Israel." *The Gerontologist* 19(5):487-95.

This study deals with the demographic analysis of the official data of suicide among the Jewish elderly in Israel as an illustration of a multicultural, pluralistic society.

KW: Elderly / Suicide

203 Shichor, D. and S. Kobrin. 1976. "Criminal Behavior among the Elderly." *The*

Gerontologist 18(2):213-18.

Points out that criminal justice agencies tend to treat elderly offenders leniently. As a largely powerless group, the elderly may well have been viewed as less than fully responsible for their criminal acts. However, their growth in relative and absolute numbers and of their political power would confront criminal justice agencies with novel problems of discriminating among impaired and competent elderly offenders.

KW: Crime / Elderly / Statistics

6

Criminal Justice

204 Bensinger, G. J. 1976. "A Practical Perspective For Criminal Justice Planning." *Police Law Quarterly* VI(1):31-5.

Discusses the proceedings of a conference on criminal justice training and education and the action steps that resulted. The purpose of the conference (held in 1975, Cook County, IL) was to bring personnel and educators together to develop relations between criminal justice agencies and higher education.

KW: Higher education / Personnel / Training / United States

205 Bensinger, G. J. 1977. "Training for Criminal Justice Personnel: A Case Study." *Federal Probation* XLI(3):31-7.

Attempted to provide corrections and court practitioners and managers with a case study of a unique and comprehensive training project that was established primarily for non-law enforcement personnel in Cook County, Illinois.

KW: Corrections / Courts / Practitioners / Training / United States

206 Bensinger, G. J. 1982. "Criminal Justice in Israel: A Research Note." *Journal of Criminal Justice* 10:393-401.

Describes the rise in crime in recent years in Israel, especially violent crime. Discusses the criminal justice system in Israel and analyzes some of the problems of law enforcement, courts, probation, and corrections there.

KW: Corrections / Courts / Crime / Law enforcement / Probation / Violent crime

207 Bensinger, G. J. 1992. *Justice in Israel: A Survey of Criminal Justice*. Chicago: Office of International Criminal Justice.

KW: Comparative research / Criminal justice

208 Bensinger, G. J. 1992. "Crime and Criminal Justice in Israel." *Criminal Justice International* 8(6):13-19.

KW: Comparative research / Criminal justice

209 Bensinger, G. J. and E. T. Crego. 1974. "Improving Criminal Justice Through Training and Development." *Judicature* 57:410-16.

Recommends the improvement of criminal justice agencies through offering training and leadership program at the agency level. Reports that within a year and a half, Cook County, Illinois, developed an excellent training program and once training capacity was reached at the agency level, the original program would revert to consulting efforts.

KW: Leadership / Training / United States

210 Bensinger, G. J. and E. T. Crego. 1975. "How Cook County Got a Comprehensive Criminal Justice Training Program: Or the Art of Muddling Through." *Illinois Issues* 1(9):62-4.

Describes how an alliance of county officials, practitioners and academics succeeded in creating, and gaining approval for, a new training program for criminal justice personnel in Cook County. Argues that the key to the success of the program was the persistence of the participants.

KW: Leadership / Training / United States

211 Bensinger, G. J. and E. A. Kazemek. 1975. "Training of Trainers: Developing Criminal Justice Trainers - A Case Study." *Training and Development Journal* 29(9):36-41.

Describes one approach to prepare a diverse group of 15 individuals, representing seven different agencies in Chicago's Cook County's criminal justice system, to assume the responsibility for planning, administering and delivering training within their respective agencies.

KW: Planning / Training / United States

212 Shichor, D., R. M. O'Brien, D. L. Decker. 1981. "Prestige of Journals in Criminology and Criminal Justice." *Criminology* 19(3):461-9.

Poole and Regoli examined the problems of measuring prestige in periodicals in criminology and criminal justice via subjective evaluations and developed an alternative to the measure of journal eminence offered by Shichor et al., based on citation frequency. Differences in journal rankings derived from these contrasting methods are assessed.

KW: Criminal justice / Criminology / Periodicals / Prestige

213 Shichor, D., R. M. O'Brien, D. L. Decker. 1983. "Periodical Prestige in Criminology and Criminal Justice." *Criminology* 21(3):457-61.

Poole and Regoli's concerns about Shichor et al.'s use of subjective ratings of prestige and of the concept of "average importance" were answered. The two data sets appeared to have resulted in similar rankings of professional journals indicating a consensus among professionals about the importance of particular journals.

KW: Criminal justice / Criminology / Periodicals / Prestige

214 Shoham, S. G. 1986. "Miscommunication Between Researchers and Administrators of Criminal Justice." *Israel Studies in Criminology* VII:172-6.

Presents a model describing the communication gap between the criminal justice researcher and the criminal justice administrator. Argues that relative success of criminal justice research depends on the ability to overcome communication problems.

KW: Communication / Courts / Interpersonal communication / Managers / Miscommunication / Prisons / Research applications / Researchers

215 Weller, Leonard. 1974. "Criminology." Pp. 175-209 in *Sociology in Israel* by Leonard Weller. Westport, CT: Greenwood Press.

KW: Criminological theories / Criminology

7

Criminology and Deviant Behavior

216 Addad, M. 1987. "Neuroticism, Extraversion and Meaning of Life: A Comparative Study of Criminals and Non-Criminals." *Personality and Individual Differences* 8(6):879-83.

Identified possible relationships between neuroticism and extroversion and the perception of the meaning of life. Argues that only in some specific cases could criminal solutions become a substitute to the meaning of life.

KW: Comparative research / Crime / Extroversion / Meaning of life / Neuroticism / Prisoners

217 Addad, M. and M. Benezech. 1982. "New Approach to the Process of Stigmatization in Criminology: The Preparatory Ground." *International Criminal Police Review* 356:66-72.

Offers a meaningful addition to Shoham's theory on social stigma by making it less deterministic and more dependent on the specific personality. Stigma would be possible only if the person would internalize it.

KW: Labeling / Personality disorders / Criminological theories

218 Addad, M., M. Benezech, M. Bourgeois and J. Yesavage. 1981. "Criminal Acts among Schizophrenics in French Mental Hospitals." *Journal of Nervous and Mental Disease* 169:289-93.

KW: Crime / France / Psychiatric hospitals / Schizophrenia

219 Addad, M. and A. Leslau. 1990. "Immoral Judgement, Extraversion, Neuroticism and Criminal Behavior." *International Journal of Offender Therapy and Comparative Criminology* 34(1):1-13.

Examines the relationship between neuroticism, immoral judgment and criminality. Positive relation between criminality and neuroticism was independent of immoral judgment; also positive relation between immoral judgement and criminality was independent of neuroticism.

KW: Crime / Extroversion / Moral judgement / Neuroticism

220 Addad, M. and S. G. Shoham. 1985. "Stigma, Creativity, Crime and Madness."

Deviant Behavior 6(1):67-81.

Deals with the notions of stigma as related to crime and madness. It expounds a new personality theory which is related to the genesis of both crime and madness and presents madness as an incentive to creativity.

KW: Creativity / Crime / Labeling / Mental disorders / Personality theories

221 Ben-Yehuda, N. 1985. *Deviance and Moral Boundaries: Witchcraft, the Occult, Science Fiction, Deviant Sciences and Scientists.* Chicago: University of Chicago Press.

Provides a wide and comprehensive theoretical framework for social deviance that focuses on social and moral boundaries. Claims that deviance is not a marginal but rather a central phenomenon that points to wider social processes of stability and change.

KW: Antisocial behavior / Crime / Deviance / Moral values / Social norms

222 Ben-Yehuda, N. 1990. *The Politics and Morality of Deviance: Moral Panics, Drug Abuse, Deviant Science, and Reserved Stigmatization.* Albany: State University of New York Press.

Presents a theory for the reciprocal relations between politics, morality and deviant behavior. Views deviance as a relative phenomenon whose meaning varies according to cultural context and moral symbols.

KW: Antisocial behavior / Case study / Crime / Criminological theories / Cultural differences / Deviance / Drug addiction / Morality / Politics

223 Bensinger, G. J. 1984. "Chicago Youth Gangs: A New-Old Problem." *Journal of Crime and Justice* II:1-16.

KW: Youth gangs

224 Bensinger, G. J. 1985. "Getting Serious About Chicago's Gang Problems." *Law Enforcement News* XI(4, February 25):8, 13.

Mentions the murder of an aspiring high school basketball star in Chicago as the catalyst for a public outcry against murders committed by gangs that received little public concern prior to that. Cited new approaches taken by the Chicago Police Department and the city administration that could be found in the establishment of the Task Force on Youth Crime Prevention to oversee neighborhood crime fighting projects.

KW: Youth gangs

225 Buck, A. J., M. Gross, S. Hakim and J. Weinblatt. 1983. "The Deterrence Hypothesis Revisited." *Regional Science and Urban Economics* 13(4):471-86.

KW: Criminological theories / Deterrence

226 Cohen, S., ed. 1971. *Images of Deviance.* New York: Penguin.

KW: Antisocial behavior / Crime / Deviance

227 Cohen, S. 1972. *Folk Devils and Moral Panics: The Creation of the Mods and Rockers*, London: MacGibbon and Kee (Second edition with new Introduction, "Symbols of Trouble." Oxford: Martin Robinson, 1980 and New York: St. Martins, 1981).

Discusses the social phenomenon known in the 1960s in England as "Mods and Rockers," juveniles on motorcycles who vandalized beaches. Suggests that the exaggerated media reaction to this stemmed paradoxically from a societal need to have deviant groups to act as defense mechanisms to the norms of the majority.

KW: Historical research / Juvenile delinquency / Public opinion / Street-corner gangs / United Kingdom / Vandalism

228 Cohen, S. 1973. "Living with Crime." *New Society* 8 (November):330-3.

Discusses how crime has become an inevitable part of modern industrial society and how, in turn, people have changed their lives and values to adapt to this situation.

KW: Crime

229 Cohen, S. 1973. "The Failures of Criminology." *The Listener* 8:622-6.

KW: Criminological theories / Criminology

230 Cohen, S. 1974. "Criminology and the Sociology of Deviance in Britain: A Recent History and a Current Report." Pp. 1-40 in *Deviance and Social Control*, edited by P. Rock and M. McIntosh. London: Tavistock.

This chapter is divided into five parts: The first identifies a number of directions in which the sociology of deviance seems to be going, the second part includes a selective review of British criminology, the third part deals with the response of British sociology to the substance of studying crime and deviance, the fourth part deals with the origins and impact of the National Deviancy Conference, and the fifth part discusses traditional criminological institutions and the newer sociology of deviance.

KW: Criminological theories / Deviance / Justice / Sociological theories / Tolerance

231 Cohen, S. 1979. "Guilt, Justice and Tolerance: Some Old Concepts for a New Criminology." Pp. 17-51 in *Deviant Interpretations*, edited by D. Downes and P. Rock. New York: Harper & Row.

Discusses development trends of modern sociological and criminological theory. Points to weaknesses and examines the feasibility of charting an agenda and strategy for a new criminological policy. Argues that criminologists need to make reference to the immediate moral and political implications of their theory and be actively involved in current policy debate.

KW: Criminological theories / Guilt / Justice / Policy / Sociological theories / Tolerance

232 Cohen, S. 1979. "How Can We Balance Justice, Guilt and Tolerance?" *New Society* 47(856):475-7.

KW: Guilt / Justice / Tolerance

233 Cohen, S. 1979. "Community Control - A New Utopia." *New Society* 47(858):609-11.

KW: Social control

234 Cohen, S. 1979. "Some Modest and Unrealistic Proposals." *New Society* 47(860):731-4.

KW: Criminological theories / Criminology

235 Cohen, S. 1979. "The Punitive City: Notes on the Dispersal of Social Control." *Contemporary Crises* 3(4):339-63.

KW: Social control

236 Cohen, S. 1981. "Footprints on the Sand: A Further Report on Criminology and the Sociology of Deviance in Britain." Pp. 220-47 in *Crime and Society: Readings in History and Theory*, compiled by M. Fitzgerald, G. McLennan and J. Pawson. London: Routledge & Kegan Paul in association with the Open University Press.

Contrasts "mainstream criminology" at the end of the 1960s with the evolution at that point of the "new deviancy" school and some of the consequent developments in the following decade.

KW: Criminology / Juvenile delinquency / United Kingdom

237 Cohen, S. 1985. *Visions of Social Control: Crime, Punishment and Classification*. Cambridge: Polity Press, and New York: B. Blackwell.

KW: Crime / Punishment / Social control

238 Cohen, S. 1985. "Criminology." Pp. 140-6 in *Encyclopaedia of the Social Sciences*. London: Routledge.

KW: Criminology

239 Cohen, S. 1986. "Community Control: To Demystify or to Reaffirm?" Pp. 127-32 in *Abolitionism: Towards a Non-Repressive Approach to Crime*, edited by H. Bianchi and R. van Swaaningen. Amsterdam: Free University of Amsterdam.

Presents an approach that proposes to weaken or eliminate the power of formal law enforcement and punishment. Offers alternatives to maintain society. Argues that some of the alternatives succeeded only because they were in the shadow of the criminal law.

KW: Crime / Social control

240 Cohen, S. 1988. *Against Criminology*, New Brunswick, NJ: Transaction Books.
This is a collection of the author's articles on various aspects of criminology. The first part is introductory and presents key concepts in criminology, historical review of its development, central themes and attempts against mainstream criminology. The second part deals with anti-criminology, new paradigms and the political meaning of crime and deviance. The third part questions the implementation of theories to reality and social policy concerning social work, culture and crime.

KW: Criminological theories / Justice / Social control / Social policy

241 Cohen, S. 1989. "The Critical Discourse on 'Social Control': Notes on the Concept as a Hammer." *International Journal of the Sociology of Law* 17(3):347-57.
Examines the concept of social control as an autonomous concept not related to crime and deviance but as one that relates to the general social order. Also discusses the ideologies behind social control (justice, treatment, welfare, reform).

KW: Ideologies / Sociolinguistics / Social control

242 Cohen, S. 1989. "Criminological Theory: From Inside Out or Outside In?" *International Annals of Criminology* 27:57-64.
Argues against Quensel, who offered to return to social sciences as the solution to the crisis in criminology. Criminology is viewed as needing to redefine its position vis-a-vis issues of social justice.

KW: Criminological theories / Criminology / Justice / Philosophy of science / Social sciences

243 Cohen, S. and A. Scull, eds. 1983. *Social Control and the State: Historical and Comparative Essays*, New York: St. Martin's Press.

KW: Comparative research / Historical research / Social control

244 Cohen, S. and L. Taylor. 1975. "From Psychopaths to Outsiders: British Criminology and the National Deviancy Conference." Pp. 3-33 in *Deviance and Control in Europe*, edited by H. Bianchi, M. Simondi, I. Taylor. London: John Wiley.
The first part deals with the history of criminology in Britain until 1971 which is known as pragmatist, inter-disciplinary and positivist. These principles served as the foundation for the development of the sociology of deviant behavior. The second part deals with the development of deviant behavior.

KW: Antisocial behavior / Crime / Criminology / Historical research /

Literature review / Research / United Kingdom

245 Cohen, S. and L. Taylor. 1978. *Escape Attempts: The Theory and Practice of Resistance to Everyday Life*, New York: Penguin.
Discusses various stresses in everyday life. Through research on prison experience, the experience of "imprisonment" in routine life was highlighted along with means of escape. Coping, anxiety, imprisonment and freedom are presented as identity shaping mechanisms.

KW: Coping behavior / Life experience / Prisons / Psychological stress

246 Cohen, S. and J. Young, eds. 1973. *The Manufacture of News: Social Problems, Deviance and the Mass Media*, London: Constable; Beverly Hills, CA: Sage. Second and revised edition, Constable and Sage, 1981.
A collection of articles on mass media and its influence on social processes. The first part discusses the selection of news, the second part deals with models and styles, and the third part deals with impact and outcomes of media.

KW: Crime / Mass media / Social problems

247 Cromer, G. 1978. "Gamblers Anonymous in Israel: A Participant Observation Study of a Self-Help Group." *International Journal of the Addictions* 13(6):1069-77.
Describes a self-help group of gamblers. Gamblers redefined identities, established associations with non-gamblers and found alternative ways to spend time.

KW: Gambling / Participant observation / Self-help groups

248 Cromer, G. 1978. "Character Assassination in the Press." Pp. 225-41 in *Deviance and Mass Media*, edited by C. Winick. Beverly Hills, CA: Sage Publications.

KW: Deviance / Press

249 Cromer, G. 1985. "The Beer Affair: Israeli Social Reaction to a Soviet Agent." *Crossroads* 15:55-75.
Analyzes the public debate following the 1961 arrest of I. Beer on charges of spying for the Soviet Union. Special attention is given to social reaction against the political leadership that was perceived as responsible.

KW: Espionage / National security / Political parties / Public opinion / Social control / Soviet Union

250 Cromer, G. 1986. "Secularization is the Root of All Evil: The Response of Ultra-Orthodox Judaism to Social Deviance." *Proceedings of the Ninth World Congress of Jewish Studies*, World Union of Jewish Studies, Jerusalem, pp. 397-404.

KW: Crime / Deviance / Ideologies / Secularization / Ultra-orthodox Jews

251 Cromer, G. 1987. "The Polluted Image: The Response of Ultra-Orthodox Judaism to Israeli Television." *Sociology and Social Research* 71(3):198-9.

KW: Stereotypes / Television / Ultra-orthodox Jews

252 Cromer, G. 1987. "Negotiating the Meaning of the Holocaust: An Observation on the Debate about Kahanism in Israeli Society." *Holocaust and Genocide Studies* 2(2):289-97.

Compares Rabbi Kahana's supporters with his detractors. Kahana used the Holocaust and its meaning to support his political ideology that espoused the prevention of another holocaust. His detractors equated his ideology with Nazism.

KW: Holocaust / Kach (political) movement / Political ideologies

253 Cromer, G. 1993. "Withdrawal and Conquest: Two Aspects of the Haredi Response to Modernity." Pp. 164-80 in *Jewish Fundamentalism in Comparative Perspective: Religion, Ideology, and the Crisis of Modernity*, edited by L. Silberstein. New York: New York University Press.

KW: Modernization / Ultra-orthodox Jews

254 Cromer, G. and A. Kraus. 1986. "For the Sake of the Party: Politics and Corruption in Israeli Football." *Israel Studies in Criminology* VII:148-56.

Analyzes "bought games" in Israeli soccer during the 1950s. Corruption was not for monetary or personal gain but scores were set in advance to glorify the political party that sponsored the team. This way the popular sport reflected the "pioneering" and "ideological" atmosphere that persisted in that period.

KW: Corruption / Politics / Soccer

255 Dinitz, S. 1983. "The Dangerous Deviant: Reflections on the Mad and the Bad." *Israel Studies in Criminology* VI:29-60.

Discusses the historical development and legal definition of "danger to the public" focusing on the sociopath, psychopath and antisocial personality that hides behind the facade of sanity.

KW: Antisocial behavior / Behavior disorders / Deviance / Juvenile delinquency / Predisposition / Recidivism

256 Fischer, H. and C. Jacobsen. 1982. "Unauthorized Strikes and Slowdowns in Israel: An Institutionalized Evasion of Institutional Rules." *British Journal of Industrial Relations* XX:342-8.

KW: Social Norms / Rule evasion / Strikes

257 Fishman, G. 1976. "The Paradoxical Effect of Labeling." *International Journal of Criminology and Penology* 4:1-7.

KW: Labeling

258 Fishman, G. 1977. "Can Labeling Be Useful?" Pp. 39-47 in *Youth Crime and Juvenile Justice: International Perspectives*, edited by P. C. Friday and V. L. Stewart. New York: Praeger.

Two questions prompted this study on the effect of labeling: (1) Did all, or even most, boys after an official contact with a legal law enforcement agency really adopt a negative self-perception? and (2) Did a negative self-perception necessarily lead to further delinquent and law-breaking behavior?

KW: Labeling / Self-perception

259 Fishman, G. 1981. "Positivism and Neo-Lombrosianism." Pp. 15-23 in *The Mad, the Bad, and the Different: Essays in Honor of Simon Dinitz*, edited by I. L. Barak-Glantz and C. R. Huff. Lexington, MA: Lexington Books.

Discusses positivism, sociological positivism and criticism of the sociological approach. Concludes that the opposition manifested by mainstream American criminology to the neobiological approach was to a large degree a response to the traditional biological claims of early constitutionalists, European traditionalists, and endocrine criminologists, which were extraordinarily obstructive and hasty. Suggested to take the road of interdisciplinary research to find answers to questions on human (deviant) behavior.

KW: Criminological theories / Neo-Lombrosianism / Positivism

260 Fishman, G., A. Rattner and G. Weimann. 1987. "The Effect of Ethnicity on Crime Attribution." *Criminology* 25(3):507-24.

Examines the influence of ethnic origin on the attribution of different types of crime to persons in pictures. Ethic origin was found to be a factor in attribution of crime. Theft was attributed to Ashkenazi Jews, armed robbery to Sephardi Jews, and rape to Arabs.

KW: Attribution / Crime / Ethnic origin / Social attitudes

261 Friday, P. C. 1983. "Patterns of Role Relationships and Crime." *Israel Studies in Criminology* VI:61-74.

KW: Crime / Role relationships

262 Geyer, F. 1983. "Psychiatric, Sociological and Ontological De-Alienation: A Systems View." *Israel Studies in Criminology* VI:75-104.

KW: De-Alienation / Ontology / Psychiatry / Sociology / System analysis

263 Groves, W. B. and G. R. Newman. 1983. "Marx, Sartre and the Resurrection of Choice in Theoretical Criminology." *Israel Studies in Criminology* VI:173-92.

KW: Criminological theories

264 Hazani, M. 1986. "A Path to Deviance: A Multi-Stage Process." *Deviant Behavior* 7(2):159-74.

Examines processes and factors that cause young children to commit delinquency. According to this examination, children arrive at crime in stages: Rebellion against father's authority, socialization with other children already connected to delinquency, and seeing adult criminals as authoritarian figures.

KW: Authoritarianism / Children / Crime / Deprived areas / Reference groups

265 Hazani, M. 1989. "The Charaka Complex: Maturation out of Delinquency in an Israeli Slum." *Journal of Contemporary Ethnography* 18:243-70.

An attempt to explain why most delinquents stopped their delinquent behavior once they reached adulthood. This ethnographic study examines reckless driving and reveals that neighborhood culture consists of several age groups with adolescents rebelling and easing their way into adulthood at the same time.

KW: Correctional rehabilitation / Deprived areas / Juvenile delinquency / Reckless driving

266 Hazani, M. 1989. "Deviant Companionship and Interaction across an Intergroup 'Seam': Arab Pimps and Jewish Prostitutes." *Plural Societies* 19:55-72.

Noting that in Jerusalem the pimps are Arabs but their prostitutes are Jewish girls, this study describes and accounts for the above association and demonstrates the similarity between the Israeli phenomenon and other phenomena occurring in other plural societies.

KW: Arabs in Israel / Deviance / Jews / Pimps / Prostitution

267 Hazani, M. 1991. "The Universal Applicability of the Theory of Neutralization: German Youth Coming to Terms with the Holocaust." *Crime, Law and Social Change* 15:135-49.

This is an empirical study of German youth, born after the Second World War. The study focuses on how they cope with crimes committed by the Nazi regime. The study utilizes Sykes and Matza's techniques of guilt neutralization to explain how coping was done.

KW: Germany / Holocaust / Values / Young adults

268 Jacobsen, C. 1974. "The Permissive Society and Its Victims: A Preliminary Statement." *International Journal of Criminology and Penology* 2:173-9.

KW: Conformity / Criminological theories / Deviance / Permissiveness

269 Jacobsen, C. 1979. "Permissiveness and Norm Evasions: Definitions, Relationships, and Implications." *Sociology* 13(2):219-33.

Distinguishes between permissiveness and weakening of norms. Defines relevant concepts and their contribution for the functioning of a normative system. This model is based on collective behavior where permissive societies develop functional alternatives to social control or risk disintegration.

KW: Collective behavior / Conformity / Models / Permissiveness / Social control / Social norms / Social structure / Social systems

270 Jacobsen, C. 1983. "What it Means to be Considerate: Differences in Normative Expectations and their Implications." *Israel Social Science Research* 1(1):24-33.

Explores differences in being considerate based on cultural attributes. Pointed to dangers of misinterpretation of cues that may lead to increase in violence and decrease in being considerate. Children of Middle Eastern parents described significantly more responsive acts and less spontaneous acts than children of Western parents. The authors used these findings for predicting aggressive behavior.

KW: Aggressive behavior / Content analysis / Cooperation / Cultural differences / Elementary school age / Ethnic origin / Social behavior

271 Jacobsen, C. 1988/9. "Expecting Consideration: Further Insights - A Research Note." *Israel Social Science Research* 6(2):83-6.

The study aimed to test the hypothesis that visible lack of consideration in Israeli society stemmed from cultural differences between East and West regarding the concept of consideration.

KW: Aggressive behavior / Content analysis / Cooperation / Cultural differences / Elementary school age / Ethnic origin / Interpersonal relations / Media / Social behavior

272 Jacobsen, C. and R. Bronson. 1985. *Simulating Violators*. Baltimore, MD: Operations Research Society of America.

The book is on computer simulation usage to test and validate sociological theories about norm violators, and it has four parts. The first deals with a theory of dynamic normative systems, the second with computer simulations, the third with validation and explanation, and the fourth offers conclusions and a discussion of the theory and beyond.

KW: Conformity / Deviance / Norm evasion / Computer simulation

273 Jacobsen, C., R. Bronson. 1989. "Thank You for Not Smoking: Simulating the Growth of A New Social Norm." Pp. 531-6 in *Operational Research and the Social Sciences*, edited by M. C. Jackson, P. Keys and S. A. Cropper. New York: Plenum Press.

This is a test of the theory of normative changes in current societies with regard to smoking in public. Unlike other social norms, attitudes towards smoking had hardened, and smoking in public became less and less acceptable.

KW: Models / Simulation / Smoking / Social change / Social norms

274 Kruglansky, A. W. and Y. Yinon. 1974. "Evaluating an Immoral Act Under Threat versus Temptation: An Illustration of the Achievement Principle in Moral Judgement." *Journal of Moral Education* 3(2):167-75.

Hypothesizes that resistance of the moral idea would be judged more moral and compliance with it less immoral when: (1) the act is intended to prevent a decline in outcomes rather than to effect an improvement in outcomes, (2) the immoral idea originates in an external agent versus the potential actor, and (3) the magnitude of extrinsic inducement to commit the act is high versus low.

KW: Crime / Moral judgement / Temptation

275 Landau, S. F. and L. Sebba, eds. 1977. *Criminology in Perspective: Essays in Honor of Israel Drapkin*. Lexington, MA: Lexington Books.

This book constitutes a collection of articles in four areas: Historical and theoretical perspectives, issues in contemporary criminology, clinical theories and practice, and trends in the administration of justice.

KW: Criminological theories / Criminology / Historical research / Victimology

276 McMahon, M. and G. Kellough. 1987. "An Interview with Stanley Cohen." *Canadian Criminology Forum* 8:132-49.

KW: Criminology

277 Mednick, S. A. and W. F. Gabrielli. 1983. "Gene Environment Interactions and Crime." *Israel Studies in Criminology* VI:31-42.

KW: Crime / Genetics

278 Nachshon, I. 1982. "Toward Biosocial Approaches in Criminology." *Journal of Social and Biological Structures* 5:1-9.

Nineteen-century biological theories were rejected by sociological theories that emphasized socio-cultural factors over psychopathological ones. An argument is made here for a biosocial approach to include biological, psychological and sociological data.

KW: Crime causes / Criminality / Criminological theories / Criminology / Sociobiology

279 Nachshon, I. 1983. "Hemisphere Dysfunction in Psychopathy and Behavior Disorders." Pp. 389-414 in *Hemisyndromes: Psychobiology, Neurology, Psychiatry*, edited by M. S. Myslobodsky. New York: Academic Press.

KW: Behavior disorders / Brain damage / Comparative research / Crime

280 Rahav, G. and M. Teichman. 1984. "Assessing the Seriousness of Deviant Behaviour: The Effect of Interpersonal Resources." Pp. 161-70 in *Law and Psychology*, edited by D. J. Muller, D. E. Blackman and A. J. Chapman. New

York: Wiley.

KW: Crime / Deviance / Interpersonal resources

281 Rattner, A., G. Weimann and G. Fishman. 1990. "Cross Ethnic Identification and Misidentification by Israelis." *Sociology and Social Research* 74(2):73-9.

KW: Ethnic origin / Identification

282 Rotenberg, M. 1977. "Deviance and Contingent Beings." *Israel Studies in Criminology* IV:189-205.

Presents a model to explain criminal behavior that offered to integrate active and reactive approaches to deviant behavior. Deviance is explained as "actions" (roles) and "reactions" (labeling).

KW: Antisocial behavior / Crime causes / Labeling / Models

283 Sagarin, E. 1983. "Salvation Through Fiction." *Israel Studies in Criminology* VI:227-40.

284 Sebba, L. 1978. "The Comparative Method in Criminology." Pp. 245-65 in *Israeli Reports to the Tenth International Congress of Comparative Law*, edited by S. Goldstein, Institute for Legislative Research and Comparative Law, Jerusalem. Also published in *Israel Studies in Criminology* V:15-38, 1979.

KW: Comparative research / Criminology

285 Sharfstein, B-A. 1983. "Prehuman Intimations of Human Art." *Israel Studies in Criminology* VI:241-54.

KW: Art

286 Shichor, D. 1970. "Nonconformity Patterns of Different Types of Leaders in Small Groups." *Comparative Group Studies* 1(3):269-74.

Deals with theoretical assumptions which were derived from several small group studies and could serve to generate research which would explore the relationship between the different roles of leadership and the patterns of nonconformity attached to them in small groups.

KW: Leadership / Small groups

287 Shichor, D. 1976. "The Counter-Culture: Why was Sociology Taken by Surprise?" Pp. 182-97 in *Youth Unrest*, edited by S. G. Shoham. Jerusalem: Jerusalem Academic Press.

Addresses the criticism raised against social scientists for failing to predict the youth "counter-culture." Maintains that the reasons for this lack of foresight and prediction could be related to two different sources: to the present state of sociology as a scientific discipline and to the very nature of the new counter-culture.

KW: Counter-culture / Sociological theories

288 Shichor, D. 1980. "The New Criminology: Some Critical Issues." *British Journal of Criminology* 20(1):1-19.

Reviews several basic premises of the New Criminology and raised some issues concerning this approach. These are: theoretical oversimplification, over-politicization, opposition to reform measures, lack of theoretical and empirical concern for the totalitarian nature of "ideal" societies, over-emphasis on political activism, oversimplified view of capitalist society.

KW: Criminology / New criminology

289 Shichor, D. 1980. "Some Problems of Credibility in Radical Criminology." Pp. 191-212 in *Radical Criminology: The Coming Crisis*, edited by J. A. Inciardi. Beverly Hills, CA: Sage.

The analysis pointed out several controversial issues such as, the nature of the law, crime causation, the role of the criminologists, religious devotion and liberation, crime and revolution. The author argued that raising these questions had contributed to criminological discourse.

KW: Credibility / Criminology / Radical criminology

290 Shichor, D. 1982. "An Analysis of Citations in Introductory Criminology Textbooks: A Research Note." *Journal of Criminal Justice* 10(3)231-7.

An attempt to find out which social scientists were most cited in 20 recently published criminology textbooks. A list of 19 names of influential criminologists and some additional findings were provided.

KW: Citations / Criminology

291 Shichor, D. and R. Ellis. 1981. "Begging in Israel: An Exploratory Study." *Deviant Behavior* 2(2):109-25.

The study describes begging and the personal characteristics, career development and attitudes of beggars based upon personal interviews. Due to the Jewish tradition of charity, begging had a more positive public image than in most industrial societies. This reflected on the beggar's self-concept which was less negative.

KW: Begging / Exploratory study / Panhandling

292 Shoham, S. 1962. "The Application of the 'Culture-Conflict' Hypothesis to the Criminality of Immigrants in Israel." *The Journal of Criminal Law, Criminology and Police Science* 53(2):207-18

Sketches some findings of the American research on immigrants and then presents own findings with respect to the crime rates of immigrants who have come to Israel since 1948, the crime rates of immigrants from the various continents, the types of offenses committed by immigrants from different regions, and the "second generation" problems, concerning delinquency rates of juveniles with immigrant parents.

KW: Acculturation / Conflict / Crime / Culture / Immigrants

293 Shoham, S. G. 1965. "The Norm, the Act and the Object of Crime as Bases for the Classification of Criminal Behaviour." *The International Journal of Social Psychiatry* 11(4).

Offers a typology for classifying criminal behavior according to three components: the legal norm that had been violated, the object the act targeted, and the nature of the act. This typology is different from others in that it is not based on the criminal's history but on the type of act committed.

KW: Antisocial behavior / Crime / Measures / Social norms

294 Shoham, S. G. 1966. *Crime and Social Deviation.* Chicago: H. Regnery.

KW: Crime / Deviance

295 Shoham, S. G. 1967. "Psychopathy as Social Stigma: A Myth Revisited." *Corrective Psychiatry and Journal of Social Therapy* 13(1):21-41

Maintains that the usage of the psychiatric label "psychopath" did not serve the pure science of psychiatry but rather was used to create a stigma to define those who deviate from normative behavior. Their behavior would be labeled as such when it contradicted given social conventions. Thus the concept reflected a social sanction against the non-conformists and not a personality defect or pathological syndrome.

KW: Labeling / Mental disorders / Psychiatry / Psychological diagnosis

296 Shoham, S. G. 1968. "Culture Conflict as a Frame of Reference for Research in Criminology and Social Deviation." Pp. 55-82 in *Crime and Culture: Essays in Honor of Thorsten Sellin,* edited by M. E. Wolfgang. New York: Wiley.

KW: Acculturation / Antisocial behavior / Crime / Criminological theories / Deviance

297 Shoham, S. G. 1968. "Social Stigma and the Criminal Group: Social Stigma and the Genesis of Criminal and Deviant Subcultures." *The Irish Jurist* 3:78-100.

KW: Antisocial behavior / Criminal subculture / Labeling

298 Shoham, S. 1970. "Research in Criminology in a Country of Social Change." *Israel Studies in Criminology* I:9-34.

KW: Criminology / Research / Social change

299 Shoham, S. G. 1970. "Accidia, Anomie, Alienation and The Absurd." *Indian Journal of Social Research* XI(2):123-38.

The author suggests to revive the concepts "Accidie," "Acedy," or "Accidia" to describe the collapse of the individual's value involvement. This, in a similar fashion to the way that "Anomy," "Anomie," or

"Anomia" were revived from their common usage in the 16th century to describe society's normative collapse. This way it would be possible to focus again on the individual and not on the group.

KW: Alienation / Social norms

300 Shoham, S. G. 1970. *The Mark of Cain: The Stigma Theory of Crime and Social Deviance.* Oceana Publications, New York and Israel Universities Press. Also published in 2nd Revised Edition (with G. Rahav), University of Queensland Press. Queensland. 1982.

KW: Crime / Deviance / Labeling

301 Shoham, S. G. 1975. "The Tantalus Ratio: A Scaffolding for Some Personality-Core Vectors." *The Journal of Genetic Psychology* 126:119-44. Also published as Shoham, S. G. 1977. "The Tantalus Ratio." *Israel Studies in Criminology* IV:96-122.

Presented a theory for personality development based on "participation" and "separation."

KW: Ego / Personality development / Personality theories / Self-concept

302 Shoham, S. G. 1975. "Stigma and Stereotype - The Interactionist Approach." Pp. 39-54 in *New Perspectives in Criminology*, Verlag der Fachvereine. Also published as Shoham, S. G. 1977. "Stigma and Stereotype - The Interactionist Approach." *Israel Studies in Criminology* IV:206-33.

An attempt to delineate the changing labels of deviance as part of the explanation of stigma and the role of social stigma in generating social deviance as compared to deviant behavior and value deviation.

KW: Antisocial behavior / Labeling / Stereotypes / Violence

303 Shoham, S. G. 1976. *Social Deviance.* New York: Gardner Press.

KW: Deviance

304 Shoham, S. G. 1977. "The Isaac Syndrome." *Israel Studies in Criminology* IV:171-88.

KW: Deviance

305 Shoham, S. G. 1979. *Salvation Through the Gutters: Deviance and Transcendence.* Washington, DC: Hemisphere.

KW: Deviance

306 Shoham, S. G. 1979. "Labeling and Beyond." *Israel Studies in Criminology* V:39-68.

KW: Antisocial behavior / Labeling / Social perception

307 Shoham, S. G. 1980. "The Single-Standard Deviant." Pp. 236-50 in *Crime and Deviance: A Comparative perspective,* edited by G. R. Newman. Beverly Hills, CA: Sage Publications.

Shoham highlights correlates of social deviance which are related to his recent personality theory. Maintains that self concept, value deviation, deviant behavior, social stigma and cognitions of transcendence resulted in social deviance.

KW: Deviance

308 Shoham, S. G. 1983. "The Many Faces of Crime and Deviance." *Israel Studies in Criminology* VI:IX.

KW: Crime / Deviance / Violence

309 Shoham, S. G. 1983. *Sex as Bait: Eve, Casanova and Don Juan.* New York: University of Queensland Press.

KW: Deviance / Sex

310 Shoham, S. G. 1983. *The Violence of Silence: The Impossibility of Dialogue.* New Brunswick, NJ: Transaction Books.

KW: Deviance

311 Shoham, S. G. 1985. "Dialectical Quests as Metaphysical Projections of the Self. A Criminologist's Concept of Ultimate Reality and Meaning." *Ultimate Reality and Meaning* 8(3):196-208.

KW: Deviance / Dialectics / Meaning / Reality

312 Shoham, S. G. 1988. *The Deviant Personality: A Theory and Its Empirical Anchors.* Cambridge, MA: Brookline Publishing Co.

KW: Crime / Deviance / Personality traits

313 Shoham, S. G. and A. Grahame, eds. 1982. *Alienation and Anomie Revisited.* Tel-Aviv: Sheridan House and Ramot Publishing Co.

KW: Alienation / Anomie / Deviance

314 Shoham, S., M. Laskin and E. Segal. 1973. "Migration and Crime in Israel: A Research Proposal." *Israel Studies in Criminology* II:21-32.

The study proposes that deviant behavior of second and third generation migrants is a function of the degree of acculturation within the host society. A major factor preventing successful acculturation was culture conflict. In Israel, oriental immigrants experienced culture conflict as both intra- and inter-group pressure. The suggested research design involves the testing of group and individual acculturation of oriental immigrants.

KW: Crime / Migration

315 Shoham, S. and G. Rahav. 1968. "Social Stigma and Prostitution." *The British Journal of Criminology* 8(4):402-12.

KW: Labeling / Prostitution

316 Shoham, S. G., G. Rahav, R. Markovski, I. Ber, F. Chard, Y. Rachamin and C. Bill. 1983. "Family Variables and Stigma among Prostitutes in Israel." *Journal of Social Psychology* 120(1):57-62.

Examines family relationship and the process of family identity formation for prostitutes. Negative labeling by the father was followed by internalization, identity formation and finally by becoming a prostitute.

KW: Family relations / Labeling / Prostitution / Self-concept

317 Shoham, S. G., Z. Schwartzman, G. Rahav, R. Markowski, F. Chard and A. Edelstein. 1987. "An Instrument to Diagnose Personality Types According to the Personality Theory of Shoham." *Medicine and Law* 6:353-72.

The authors offer an instrument constructed to measure the direction and power of personality vectors according to Shoham's personality theory. Reliability of .91 and explanation of variance of 66% was achieved with the instrument.

KW: Personality measures / Personality theories / Test validation

318 Shoham, S. G. and G. Sher, eds. 1983. *The Many Faces of Crime and Deviance.* Tel-Aviv: Sheridan House and Ramot Publishing Co.

KW: Crime / Deviance / Juvenile delinquency

319 Shoham, S. G., L. Weissbrod, B. Gruber and Y. Stein. 1978. "Personality Core Dynamics and Predisposition Towards Homosexuality." *British Journal of Medical Psychology* 51:161-75. Also published as Shoham, S. G., L. Weissbrod, B. Wolf and Y. Stein. 1979. "Personality Core Dynamics and Predisposition Towards Homosexuality." *Israel Studies in Criminology* V:103-30.

A test of the hypothesis that oral fixation creates several common indicators for two homosexual types (male, female). Earlier fixation resulted in passivity while later fixation resulted in activity.

KW: Homosexuality / Personality traits

320 Silfen, P. 1985. "Clinical Criminology: An Emerging Profession." *Medicine and Law* 4:29-48.

Deals with the problematics and limits of clinical criminology and discusses the status of clinical criminologists in Israel and the world. Identifies problems with the profession's autonomy and the interface with clinical psychology and psychiatry.

KW: Clinical criminology / Criminology / Psychiatry

321 Silfen, P. 1988. "Clinical Criminology in Israel: A Specific Form of Criminology." Pp. 115-9 in *Applied Criminology*, edited by M. Goeppinger. Forum Verlag, Godesberg.

Unlike the view that criminology is a super-science that unifies basic sciences, here criminology is viewed as a basic science with several specialties of which one is clinical criminology.

KW: Criminality / Criminology / Psychiatry

322 Silfen, P., S. Ben-David, H. Heichal, R. Eshel, D. Lehman and D. Klieger. 1982. "From Psychiatry to Clinical Criminology." *Medicine and Law* 1:199-205.

Describes the changes in the last 24 years of psychiatric treatment of prisoners by the Israel Prison Service. A shift was observable from a narrow punishment orientation to a wider, more sophisticated, psychotherapeutic approach.

KW: Mental disorders / Prisoners / Psychiatry / Psychotherapy / Treatment methods

323 Silfen, P., S. Ben-David, D. Kliger, R. Eshel, C. Heichel, and D. Lehman. 1976. "Clinical Criminology in Israel." *International Journal of Offender Therapy and Comparative Criminology* 20(1):19-25.

KW: Criminology / Psychiatry

324 Spitzer, S. P. and B. R. West. 1979. "Assessment of the 'Reflective' Attitude and Typing of Criminal Offenses." *Israel Studies in Criminology* V:1-14.

KW: Offenses / Typology

325 Tennenbaum, Abraham N. 1992. "The Crisis in Criminology." *Telos* 92:51-62.

Argued that criminology failed not because of lack of data or theories but because of its attempt to answer the wrong questions.

KW: Criminology

326 Teichman, M. 1977. "Affiliative Behaviors among Soldiers During War Time." *British Journal of Social and Clinical Psychology* 16:3-7.

Analyzes social interactions among soldiers during war based on Shechter's affiliation theory and Foa's interpersonal resources theory. Found informal and intimate relations that started as information exchange and developed into friendship, and support.

KW: Affiliation need / Soldiers / Stress situations / War influences

327 Teichman, M. and U. G. Foa. 1972. "Depreciation and Accusation Tendencies: Empirical Support." *Journal of Individual Psychology* 28:45-50.

KW: Deviance / Social psychology

328 Weimann, G., G. Fishman and A. Rattner. 1986. "Social Distance and Misidentification." *International Journal of Comparative Sociology* 27(3-4):217-25.

KW: Arabs in Israel / Canada / Comparative research / Ethnic stereotypes / National identity / Social distance

329 Weller, L. H. Costeff, B. Cohen and D. Rahman. 1983. "Perception of Retardation and Parental Guilt Feelings." *Israel Studies in Criminology* VI:255-64.

KW: Guilt feelings / Mental retardation / Parents

330 Yesavage, J. A., M. Benezech, P. Ceccaldi, M. Bourgeois, and M. Addad. 1983. "Arson in the Mentally Ill and Criminal Populations." *Journal of Clinical Psychiatry* 4:128-30.

KW: Arson / Crime / Mentally ill

331 Yinon, Y. 1979. "Perceived Deprivation of Material and Nonmaterial Rewards as Related to Altruistic Behavior among Young Adolescents." *International Journal of Behavioral Development* 2(3):287-95.

According to this study, those who felt more deprived (materially and non-materially) demonstrated a greater propensity to respond to requests for assistance from others than those who felt less deprived.

KW: Adolescents / Altruism / Deprivation / Rewards

332 Yinon, Y., A. Abend, and A. Chirer. 1976. "Prejudice towards Israelis of Oriental Origin among Israelis of Western Origin." *Journal of Social Psychology* 99:171-8.

Subjects assessed (photos of) "westerners" more positively than "easterners," women more than men. There was interaction between gender and ethnic origin.

KW: Ethnic origin / Gender differences / Prejudice / Social perception

333 Yinon, Y., and A. Bizman. 1974. "The Nature of Affective Bonds and the Degree of Personal Responsibility as Determinants of Risk Taking for 'Self and Others.'" *Bulletin of the Psychonomic Society* 4(2A):80-2.

A tested of the hypotheses that (1) the nature of affective bonds among group members, and (2) the degrees of personal responsibility for decisions made for "self and others" were determinants of the level of risk taken in making these decisions. No interaction was found between the two variables.

KW: Affective bonds / Responsibility / Risk taking

334 Yinon, Y., M. Dovrat, and A. Avni. 1981. "The Reciprocity-Arousing Potential of the Requester's Occupation and Helping Behavior." *Journal of Applied Social Psychology* 11(3):252-8.

Examines the help requester's occupational status and the willingness to provide assistance. It was found that the occupational background has a significant impact on the willingness to help.

KW: Helping behavior / Occupational status

335 Yinon, Y., I. Sharon, Y. Gonen, and R. Adam. 1982. "Escape from Responsibility and Help in Emergencies among Persons Alone or Within Group." *European Journal of Social Psychology* 12(3):301-5.

Explores the behavior of individuals and groups in emergency situations. Groups assisted more than individuals. When responsibility could be avoided, assistance was provided in greater frequency without significant differences between groups and individuals.

KW: Altruism / Group behavior / Stress situations

336 Yinon, Y., V. Shoham, and T. Lewis. 1974. "Risky Shift in a Real vs. Role-Played Situation." *Journal of Social Psychology* 93:137-8.

KW: Risk taking / Role playing

337 Yuchtman-Yaar, E. and G. Rahav. 1986. "Resisting Small Temptations in Everyday Transactions." *Journal of Social Psychology* 126(1):23-30.

A tested of gender and age differences as to being tempted to keep excessive change for bus fare. Most subjects returned the overage; women succumbed to low temptations while men resisted higher-level temptations.

KW: Gender differences / Temptation

8

Fear of Crime

338 Farley, F. H., A. Cohen, J. Goldberg and Y. Yinon. 1978. "Fears in American and Israeli Women." *Journal of Social Psychology* 106:17-24.

Compares American and Israeli female students on a scale of fear, the scope and magnitude of fear and generalization of fear beyond a wide range of stimuli. Some differences are reported.

KW: Comparative research / Fear / United States / Women

339 Goldberg, J., Y. Yinon and A. Cohen. 1975. "A Factor Analysis of the Israeli Fear Survey Inventory." *Psychological Reports* 36:175-9.

KW: Factor analysis / Fear / Survey

340 Goldberg, J., Y. Yinon and A. Cohen. 1975. "A Cross Cultural Comparison Between the Israeli and American Fear Survey Inventory." *Journal of Social Psychology* 97:131-2.

KW: Comparative research / Cultural differences / Fear / Survey / United States

9

Homicide, Aggression, and Violence

341 Addad, M. 1983. "Violence from an Integrative Viewpoint." *Israel Studies in Criminology* VI:1-28.

Deals with violence as an integral part of everyday life in modern society. Reviewed the physiological, personality, and social sources of violent behavior. Violence is viewed as serving the human organism.

KW: Animals / Learning processes / Violence

342 Banitt, R., S. Katznelson and S. Streit. 1970. "The Situational Aspects of Violence." *Israel Studies in Criminology* I:241-58.

KW: Situational aspects / Violence

343 Cohen, S. 1966. "Vandalism." *New Education* 2:10-16.

KW: Vandalism

344 Cohen, S. 1968. "The Politics of Vandalism?" *New Society* 12 (December):872-8. Reprinted in *Juvenile Delinquency, The Family and the Social Group*, edited by J. Mays. London: Longman, 1972; and in *Society Today* 10, February, 1977.

Offers a diagnosis of vandalism in an attempt to debunk it as a mysterious crime. Argues that before any prescriptions for alleviation were provided, they needed to rely on diagnosis.

KW: Politics / Vandalism

345 Cohen, S. 1969. "Ideological and Criminal Violence." *Phalanx* 2:3-8.

KW: Criminal violence / Ideological violence / Violence

346 Cohen, S. 1973. "Campaigning Against Vandalism." Pp. 215-57 in *Vandalism*, edited by C. Ward. London: Architectural Press.

Suggests that social problems could be studied by concentrating on the ways in which society sees a certain condition as threatening or in some way counter to its interests, and then decides that something should be done about it. With this approach the author focuses on the subjective elements in the awareness of vandalism as a problem and the attempts to control or prevent it.

KW: Social reaction / Vandalism

347 Cohen, S. 1973. "Property Destruction: Motives and Meanings." Pp. 23-53 in *Vandalism*, edited by C. Ward. London: Architectural Press.

Maintains that vandalism is neither a precise behavioral description, nor a recognizable legal category, but a label attached to certain types of behavior under certain conditions. Deals with vandalism as institutionalized rule-breaking, with vandalism as a label, with motives and meaning of conventional vandalism, and with vandalism as manufactured malice and excitement.

KW: Behavior / Motives / Vandalism

348 Cohen, S. 1973. "Some Sociological Problems in the Study of Adolescent Violence." *Proceedings of the Royal Society of Medicine* 66:1131-2.

Attempts to draw the attention of a predominantly psychiatric and medical audience to some of the perspectives in recent sociological work on adolescent violence. Discusses four sociological themes which seem most challenging to the mainstream psychiatric writing in the field.

KW: Adolescents / Psychiatry / Violence

349 Cohen, S. 1974. "Breaking Out, Smashing Up and the Social Context of Aspiration." *Working Papers in Cultural Studies* 5:37-63. Reprinted in pp. 257-78 in *The Children of Ishmael: Critical Perspectives on Juvenile Justice*, edited by B. Krisberg and J. Austin. Palo Alto, CA: Mayfield, 1978.

Argues that the adolescent who commits acts of violence or vandalism, is the archetypal repository of the large fund of moral indignation which societies have in reserve. The constellation of action which is difficult to understand, let alone sympathize with, and actors who belong to a group of low power with high visibility and vulnerability, ensures that the whole battery of fantasy and mythology will be invoked to comprehend this action and justify certain forms of social control against it.

KW: Aspiration / Social context / Vandalism

350 Cohen, S. 1984. "Sociological Approaches to Vandalism." Pp. 51-63 in *Vandalism: Behavior and Motivation*, edited by C. Levy-Leboyer. Amsterdam: North Holland.

KW: Sociological theories / Vandalism

351 Cromer, G. 1979. "Football Hooliganism in England." *Israel Studies in Criminology* V:157-78.

Presents four major approaches to explain soccer hooliganism in England. Analysis focuses on types of people involved, soccer dynamics, the changing class structure and the general English social inequality.

KW: Hooliganism / Soccer / Sports violence / United Kingdom

352 Erez, E. 1986. "Intimacy, Violence and the Police." *Human Relations* 39(3):265-81.

KW: Police / Violence

353 Fishman, G., A. Rattner and V. Kraus. 1984. "Urban Communities Characteristics and the Rate of Violence in Israel." *Israel Social Science Research* 2(2):33-41.

A study of the relationships between violence, socioeconomic and demographic variables in Israeli cities. In a regression analysis it was found that internal migration is an excellent predictor of violence rates.

KW: Crime / Internal migration / Socioeconomic status / Urban areas / Violence

354 Gottlieb, B. 1976. "Frustration and Aggression Patterns of Problematic Boys on the Rosenzweig Picture-Frustration Study." *Israel Studies in Criminology* III:181-207.

KW: Frustration / Aggression

355 Horowitz, T. 1992. "Gender Plus Aggression: Gender and Other Social Variables." *Education and Society* 10(1):63-70.

Reports significant differences between the two genders on violent behavior, norms, and values connected to violence. This difference depended on social class and type of school. Vocational school students were more violent than high school students.

KW: Adolescents / Aggression / Gender differences / High schools / School violence / Social values / Socioeconomic background / Vocational schools

356 Horowitz, T. and V. Kraus. 1987. "Violence at School, Situational Factors or Societal Input." *School Psychology International* 8(2-3):141-7.

Compares three explanations given for violence in schools: a result of violence in the surrounding environment, a reaction to frustration and alienation from school, a result of already existing school violence. Frustration and alienation were not found as influencing school violence.

KW: Adolescents / Crime causes / High schools / School violence / Situational factors

357 Jaffe, Y., N. Shapir, and Y. Yinon. 1981. "Aggression and Its Escalation." *Journal of Cross-Cultural Psychology* 12(1):21-36. Also published as pp. 309-22 in *The Soviet Man in an Open Society,* edited by T. Horowitz, Lanham, University Press of America.

Compares aggression in the action of individuals and groups. Groups were found to be more aggressive than individuals and escalation of aggression is more rapid in groups than in individuals. No significant ethnic differences were found.

KW: Aggression / Caucasus / Ethnic origin / Ethnic stereotypes / Gruzia / Immigrants / Group behavior / Soviet Union

358 Jaffe, Y. and Y. Yinon. 1979. "Retaliatory Aggression in Individuals and Groups." *European Journal of Social Psychology* 9(2):177-86.
Compares aggression by individuals and groups. Group aggression was found to be more extreme than that of individuals even when there was no difference in anger level.

KW: Aggression / Decision making / Experiment / Group behavior

359 Jaffe, Y. and Y. Yinon. 1983. "Collective Aggression: The Group-Individual Paradigm in the Study of Collective Antisocial Behavior." Pp. 267-75 in *Small Groups: Social-Psychological Processes, Social Action and Living Together*, edited by H. Blumberg, P. Hare, V. Kent and M. Davies. New York: John Wiley & Sons.

KW: Aggression / Antisocial behavior / Collective aggression

360 Landau, S. F. 1974. "Type of Homicide and Pathologies Among Homicide Offenders: Some Cultural Profiles." Pp. 35-47 in *Crime and Delinquency: Dimensions of Deviance*, edited by M. Riedel and T. P. Thornberry. New York: Praeger Publishing Co. Also published in *British Journal of Criminology* 15(2):157-66, 1975.

KW: Cultural profiles / Homicide / Offender / Pathology / Typology

361 Landau, S. F. 1981. "Comment on G. M. Kressel, Sororicide Filiacide: Homicide for Family Honor." *Current Anthropology* 22(2):154-5.

KW: Bedouins / Homicide / Honor

362 Landau, S. F. 1984. "Trends in Violence and Aggression: A Cross-Cultural Analysis." *International Journal of Comparative Sociology* 25(3-4):133-58.
A cross-cultural comparison of violence and aggression based on a theoretical framework that assumes that such behaviors are reactions to stress situations when social support systems weaken.

KW: Comparative research / Criminality / Family / Inflation / Secondary data analysis / Stress situations / Violence

363 Landau, S. F. 1989. "Family Violence and Violence in Society." Pp. 25-33 in *Crime and Its Victims: International Research and Public Policy Issues*, edited by E. C. Viano. New York: Hemisphere Publishing Corporation.
Dealing with violence in the family and society, the chapter focuses on the need for increasing awareness that violence is not private but was social, on

its level and characteristics in different countries, and on intergeneration transfer of violence.

KW: Family violence / Intergenerational transmission / Social support / Violence

364 Landau, S. F. and B. Beit-Hallahmi. 1983. "Israel: Aggression in Psychohistorical Perspective." Pp. 261-86 in *Aggression in Global Perspective*, edited by A. P. Goldstein and M. H. Segall. N.Y.: Pergamon Press.

Based on perceiving aggression as a reaction to stress and tension under weakening social support, this study analyzes violence and aggression in Israel since 1948.

KW: Aggression / Stress situations / War influences / Violence

365 Landau, S. F. and D. Pfeffermann. 1988. "A Time Series Analysis of Violent Crime and Its Relation to Prolonged States of Warfare: The Israeli Case." *Criminology* 26:489-504.

Examines the influence of stressors related to wars and to lengthy war conditions on patterns of violent crime. Assumes a decrease in violent crime during increase of security-related tensions and legitimation and adjustment that predict increase in violent crime during wars.

KW: Crime / Homicide / Stress situations / Thefts / Time series analysis / Violence / War influences

366 Marx, E. 1973. "Coercive Violence in Official-Client Relationships." *Israel Studies in Criminology* II:33-68.

KW: Coercion / Violence

367 Marx, E. 1977. "Personal Violence as Social Behavior." *Israel Studies in Criminology* IV:41-66.

KW: Social behavior / Violence

368 Nachshon, I. 1986. "Hemisphere Function in Violent Offenders." Pp. 55-67 in *Biological Contributions to Crime Causation*, edited by T. E. Moffitt and S. A. Mednick. Dordrecht, The Netherlands: Martinus Nijhoff Publishers.

A test of the hypothesis (by Hare and McPherson) that recognition of nonverbal stimuli, even when processed analytically, should not be impaired in psychopaths and perhaps other violent subjects, since their deficit is assumed to be language-specific. The results seem to suggest that violent subjects suffered from a general left hemisphere dysfunction which may or may not be associated with low level arousal.

KW: Hemispheral dominance / Offender / Stimuli / Violence

369 Nachshon, I. 1990. "Neurological Bases of Crime, Psychopathy and Aggression." Pp. 194-203 in *Crime in Biological, Social, and Moral Contexts*, edited by L.

Ellis and H. Hoffman. New York: Praeger.

Focuses on the part of the brain known as the neocortex and the role it may play in criminality and in closely related behavior. Discusses the relationship between aggressive behavior and emotional arousal, reviews research which suggested that the two hemispheres contribute differently to the control of criminal behavior, especially some of its most violent and impulsive forms, and points to some issues involved in surgical control of aggression.

KW: Aggression / Crime / Neuropsychology / Psychopathy

370 Nachshon, I. 1991. "Neuropsychology of Violent Behavior: Controversial Issues and New Developments in the Study of Hemisphere Function." Pp. 93-116 in *Neuropsychology of Aggression*, edited by J. S. Milner. Boston: Kluwer Academic Publishers.

Focuses on selected controversial issues and new findings in the neuropsychological literature that are relevant to hypothesis linking violent behavior to hemisphere functions.

KW: Hemisphere function / Neuropsychology / Violence

371 Nachshon, I. and D. Denno. 1987. "Violent Behavior and Cerebral Hemisphere Function." Pp. 185-217 in *The Causes of Crime: New Biological Approaches,* edited by S. A. Mednick, T. E. Moffitt and S. A. Stack. Cambridge, NY: Cambridge University Press.

Relates violent behavior to left hemisphere disfunction, hypothesizing that left eye, arm and leg would be more dominant among violent offenders. Findings corroborated the hypothesis.

KW: Crime / Hemispheral dominance / Neuropsychology / United States / Violence

372 Rahav, G. 1983. "Homicide and Death Penalty: A Cross-Sectional Time Series Analysis." *International Journal of Comparative and Applied Criminal Justice* 7(1):61-71.

KW: Death penalty / Homicide / Time series analysis

373 Rahav, G. 1990. "Cross-National Variations in Violence." *Aggressive Behavior* 16(2):69-76.

Discussion of the hypothesis that stated a positive relation between modernization and property offenses but a negative relation between modernization and violent offenses. Maintains that in modern societies lethal aggression would be internal (suicide) more than violence directed at others.

KW: Aggression / Modernization / Suicide / Thefts / Violence

374 Rokach, A. 1989. "Anger and Aggression Control Training: An Innovative Approach in Group Psychotherapy." Pp. 198-200 in *Adolescents in Secure*

Settings, edited by R. Roberts. Toronto, Ontario, Canada: Thistletown Foundation.

Discusses Anger and Aggression Control Training (AACT) which was partly based on Novaco's stress inoculation model and partly on Meichenbaum's theoretical conceptualizations. The anger and aggression control procedures intervened at both cognitive and behavioral levels and included three phases: awareness and cognitive structuring, coping skills training, and evaluation and readjustment.

KW: Aggression / Anger / Group therapy / Stress / Training

375 Rubin, R. 1983. "The Psychobiology of Human Aggression and Violence." *Israel Studies in Criminology* VI:205-26.

Discusses the psychophysiological causes for human aggression and violence. The morphological and functional development of the central nervous system was subject to androgenous hormones. Post-partum abnormality (due to exposure to drugs) may precipitate violent outbursts. However some behavior was seen due to learned/acquired traits not only innate ones.

KW: Aggression / Psychophysiology / Violence

376 Schwarzwald, J. and Y. Yinon. 1978. "Physical Aggression: Effects of Ethnicity of Target and Directionality of Aggression." *European Journal of Social Psychology* 8:367-76.

KW: Aggression / Ethnicity / Prejudice

377 Shoham, S. G. 1969. "Points of No Return: Some Situational Aspects of Violence." *The Prison Journal* 48(2):29-33.

An attempt to explain the criminal act by a situational approach that views violent crime as a deterioration of a given set of relationships. Participants' background in the situation was less relevant than the chain of events that lead to it. It adopts a "point of no return."

KW: Crime / Crime causes / Delinquency prevention / Violence

378 Shoham, S., S. Ben-David, and G. Rahav. 1974. "Interaction in Violence." *Human Relations* 27(5):417-30.

Examines the actual process of eruption of the violent act. Concentrates on a stimulus-response interaction and examines the nature of the provocation, the nature of the reaction, and the relationship between the two factors. These three components constitute one cycle, and each cycle acts as a stimulus to the subsequent one.

KW: Stimulus-response / Violence

379 Shoham S., S. Ben-David, R. Vadmani, J. Atar and S. Fleming. 1973. "The Cycles of Interaction in Violence." *Israel Studies in Criminology* II:69-87.

KW: Violence

380 Teichman, M. 1989. "The Prediction of Marital Violence." Pp. 315-25 in *Social Applications and Issues in Psychology*, Vol. 8, edited by R. C. King, and J. K. Collins. Amsterdam: Elsevier.

Classifies and predicts violent situations between family members in a marriage setting as a resource exchange. Violent behavior is seen as a form of interpersonal behavior.

KW: Behavior prediction / Family relations / Family violence / Marriage / Needs / Resources

381 Teichman, M. and Y. Teichman. 1989. "Violence in the Family: An Analysis in Terms of Interpersonal Resource-Exchange." *Journal of Family Violence* 4(2):127-42.

Spouse abuse is reviewed within the framework of interpersonal relations and analyzed as exchange of resources. An attempt to predict violence as a channel of exchange.

KW: Family intervention / Family violence / Marital relations

382 Weller, L., I. Glantz and I. Klein. 1973. "Personality Characteristics of First-Time Offenders and Recidivists and of Property and Violent Offenders." *Israel Studies in Criminology* II:113-24.

KW: First-time offenders / Personality traits / Property offenses / Recidivism / Violent offenders

383 Yinon, Y., Y. Jaffe, and S. Feshbach. 1975. "Risky Aggression in Individuals and Groups." *Journal of Personality and Social Psychology* 31(5):808-15.

KW: Aggression / Groups / Individuals

10

Juvenile Delinquency and Juvenile Justice

384 Addad, M. and M. Benezech. 1979. "Schizophrenia and Delinquency." *Israel Studies in Criminology* V:69-102.

KW: Juvenile delinquency / Schizophrenia

385 Addad, M. and M. Benezech. 1981. "Mental Retardation: Diagnosis and Delinquency." *Indian Journal of Criminology & Criminalistics* 1(4):134-40.

Contrary to prevailing assumptions, this study found that the percentage of mental retardation among criminals was only slightly higher than among the general population. The authors argue that deviance of mentally ill may be due to their difficulty in adjusting with the immediate environment, suggestibility and other reasons, and that they fall prey to the exploitation of normal persons. Due to retardation, their ability to evade apprehension was also low. No direct relationship between retardation and criminality was established.

KW: Juvenile delinquency / Mental retardation

386 Amir, M. 1966. *Community Action Programmes for the Control and Prevention of Delinquency: A Critical Analysis of the Literature with Special Reference to Israel*, Jerusalem, Israel: Ministry of Welfare.

The report offers a historical view, analytical perspective, and a discussion of why programs failed. It then describes target communities and groups, offered a planning orientation, theoretical and etiological roots of delinquency. The report focuses on the community, the individual, groups, family, schools, employment, police and on the role of research and evaluation in the provision of community-based programs.

KW: Delinquency prevention

387 Amir, M. 1976. "The Conflict of Cultures and Subcultures - The Changing Concept of Ghetto Youth: An Overview." Pp. 198-218 in *Youth Unrest*, edited by S. G. Shoham. Jerusalem: Jerusalem Academic Press.

Discusses the changing scene of ghetto youth. Maintains that a new reaction, or theme, had been observed - the politicization of the ghetto youth due to major changes within the ghetto. The most important changes were the youths' demands to control their own lives and environment, and to be accorded the possibility to leave the situations of marginality and to achieve social worth.

KW: Conflict / Culture / Ghetto youth / Subculture

388 Amir, M. and M. Hovav. 1970. "Juvenile Delinquency in Israel." Pp. 465-96 in *Children and Families in Israel: Some Mental Health Perspectives*, edited by A. Jarus, J. Marcus, J. Oren and C. Rapaport, London: Gordon and Breach.
Reviews matters related to the epidemiology of delinquency, causes, societal reaction, services and problems in service delivery (or lack of).

KW: Authorities / Causes / Definitions / Juvenile delinquency / Juvenile prison / Pre-delinquent services / Statistics / Urbanization

389 Amir, M. and M. Hovav. 1976. "Juvenile Delinquency in Israel (Major Trends in Statistical Data)." *Israel Annals of Psychiatry and Related Disciplines* 14(2):161-72.
The purpose of the study was to identify five-year development patterns in juvenile delinquency in Israel. Found that worsening of social conditions was associated with a rise in marginality and delinquency-causing conditions.

KW: Ethnic status / Juvenile delinquency / Secondary data analysis / Socioeconomic status

390 Arieli, M., J. Beker and Y. Kashti. 1990. "Residential Group Care as a Socializing Environment: Toward a Broader Perspective." *Child and Youth Care Services* 13(1):45-58.
This study deals with types of boarding schools. Education in boarding schools was commonly perceived as contrary to optimal education that is geared towards children at risk. Some boarding schools were perceived as shaping leadership of elite youth. The authors discuss this contrast.

KW: Boarding schools / Elites / Social mobility / Social structure / Socialization / Youth in distress

391 Arieli, M. and Y. Kashti. 1977. "The Socially Disadvantaged Peer Group in the Israeli Residential Setting." *Jewish Journal of Sociology* 19(2):145-55.
Describes residential education in Israel. Approximately 18% of Jewish children ages 13-17 were in 350 residential institutions, the highest percentage in the world. Discusses type, structures, and goals of residential settings.

KW: Adolescents / Aliyat Ha'no'ar (youth immigration) / Culturally disadvantaged youth / Peers / Residential settings

392 Banitt, R., R. Feder, E. Segal and J. Smilansky. 1970. "The Etiology of Middle-Class Delinquency in Israel." *Israel Studies in Criminology* I:119-40.

KW: Juvenile delinquency / Middle-class

393 Bensinger, G. J. 1984. "Juvenile Delinquency Prevention and Control in Israel. *Federal Probation* 48(4):66-70.
Discusses the increase in scope and seriousness of juvenile delinquency in Israel and legal and other reactions to it. Presents statistics on delinquency and some salient cases to illustrate the situation.

KW: Juvenile delinquency

394 Bensinger, G. J. 1990. "The Juvenile Court of Cook County: Past, Present and Future." *Journal of Crime and Justice* 13(2):105-24.
Presents a brief historical narration and an analysis of some of the problems affecting the Juvenile Court of Cook County - the United States' first. Concludes that though undergoing some fundamental changes, it was not endangered and as such may continue the tradition begun in Chicago 100 years ago.

KW: Juvenile court / United States

395 Bensinger, G. J. 1990. "The Citizen's Committee on the Juvenile Court of Cook County: A Case Study of Informing and Influencing Policy Makers." *Perspectives* 14(2):26-30.
Traces the historic development of the Cook County juvenile justice system and examines some of the benefits and policy changes produced by citizen participation in governmental affairs over a period of 25 years.

KW: Juvenile court / Juvenile justice / United States

396 Berg, D. and D. Shichor. 1977. "Methodological and Theoretical Issues in Juvenile Diversion: Implications for Evaluations." Pp. 749-66 in *Deviant Behavior*, edited by D. H. Kelly. New York: St. Martin's Press.
This study offers an evaluation of the Behavioral Assessment and Treatment Services Center in Orange County, California. It was found to be no better or worse than its counterparts in the juvenile justice system.

KW: Diversion

397 Cohen, Y. 1965. "Prevention of Delinquency in Israel." Pp. 165-75 in *The Prevention of Crime and the Treatment of Offenders in Israel*, A Report to the Third UN Congress on the Prevention of Crime and the Treatment of Offenders, Stockholm, August 9 to 18, Jerusalem, Israel: Government Printer.

KW: Delinquency prevention

398 Cohen, S. 1967. "Mods, Rockers and the Rest: Community Reactions to Juvenile Delinquency." *Howard Journal of Penology and Crime Prevention* 12(2):121-30. Also published as pp. 273-84 in *Juvenile Delinquency, the Family and the Social Group*, edited by J. B. Mays. London: Longman, 1972; and in *Crime and Delinquency in Britain*, edited by W. G. Carson and P. Wiles. Martin

Robertson, 1974.

KW: Juvenile delinquency / Mods / Rockers / United Kingdom

399 Cohen, S. 1971. "Directions for Research in Adolescent Group Violence and Vandalism." *British Journal of Criminology* 11(4):319-40.

KW: Adolescents / Group violence / Research / Vandalism / Violence

400 Cohen, S. 1973. "Protest, Unrest and Delinquency: Convergence in Labels and Behaviour." *International Journal of Criminology* 1(2). Also published as pp. 278-94 in *Youth Unrest*, edited by S. G. Shoham. Jerusalem: Jerusalem Academic Press.

Discusses problems raised by the blurring of the boundary lines between action usually labeled as "protest," "unrest," "dissent," and delinquency. Focuses specifically on violent or disruptive behavior.

KW: Behavior / Juvenile delinquency / Labeling / Protest / Unrest

401 Cohen, S. and D. Dery. 1984. "On Defining Juvenile Delinquency as a Policy Problem." Pp. 37-53 in D. Dery, *Problem Definition in Policy Analysis*. Lawrence, KS: University Press of Kansas.

KW: Juvenile delinquency / Policy

402 Cohen, S. and P. Rock. 1970. "The Teddy Boy." Pp. 288-320 in *The Age of Affluence: 1951-1964*, edited by V. Bogdanor and R. Skidelsky. London: Macmillan.

Discusses juveniles who demanded most out of leisure but for whom the least was offered. Delinquency arose from this type of discontinuity and frustration. It was the response to the setting of impossibly high leisure aspirations which arose from the previous dissociation from work and school achievements. Although the delinquent solution took place in the field of leisure, the problem it solved went further back into the social structure.

KW: Juvenile delinquency / Leisure / Teddy Boy

403 Cromer, G. 1976. "The Israeli Black Panthers: Fighting for Credibility and a Cause." *Victimology* 1(3):403-13.

KW: Black Panthers / Protest

404 Cromer, G. 1978. "The Israeli Black Panthers: A Case Study of the Politicisation of Juvenile Delinquents." *Howard Journal of Penology and Crime Prevention* 17(1):41-8.

Argues that the (Israeli) Black Panthers' delinquent past had haunted them ever since they decided to enter the political arena. They battled on two fronts, defending their own identity and attacking that of their opponents. The debate had centered on the politicization process itself rather than the ends it was meant to serve.

KW: Black Panthers / Juvenile delinquency

405 Cromer, G. 1978. "Drama as Catharsis and Catalyst: Two Ways of Preventing Delinquency." *International Journal of Offender Therapy and Comparative Criminology* 22(1):91-6.

KW: Drama / Delinquency prevention

406 Cromer, G. 1978. "Linguistic Aspects of Transformative Labelling: The Case of Repentant Delinquents." *Mental Health and Society* 5(3-4):186-93.

KW: Labeling / Religious repentance / Religious rhetoric

407 Cromer, G. 1981. "Repentant Delinquents: A Religious Approach to Rehabilitation." *Jewish Journal of Sociology* 23(2):113-22.

Analyzes the process that was used to rehabilitate criminals through religious repentance and possible reasons for success of this approach. Proselytes underwent a complete change in their identity as criminals, but maintained the dichotomy between them and society.

KW: Criminality / Jerusalem / Rehabilitation / Religious repentance

408 Cromer, G. 1988. "Sad Tales and Happy Tales: The Politicization of Delinquent Life Histories." *Political Communication and Persuasion* 5(3):179-90.

This study is based on life histories of two groups of Israeli delinquents, and it suggests that they sometimes engaged in a particular kind of retrospective interpretation (of their dismal past and their portrayal of themselves as victims) in order to bring about far reaching changes. It was aimed at influencing the decision as to the appropriate agents of social contacts, and it constituted part of a wider struggle for political and cultural legitimacy.

KW: Biographies / Juvenile delinquency

409 Donnenwerth, G. V., M. Teichman, and U. G. Foa. 1973. "Cognitive Differentiation of Self and Parents in Delinquent and Nondelinquent Girls." *British Journal of Social and Clinical Psychology* 12:144-52.

KW: Cognitive differences / Female adolescents / Juvenile delinquency / Parents / Self-perception

410 Eisenstadt, S. N. 1976. "The Harassed Society - Generational Conflict: Intellectual Trends and Institutional Responses in Contemporary Society." Pp. 116-39 in *Youth Unrest*, edited by S. G. Shoham. Jerusalem: Jerusalem Academic Press.

Suggests that part of the explanation of the new features of youth rebellion and student protest lied in the convergence and mutual reinforcement of the two major sets of conditions and processes - namely, of widespread intellectual antinomianism on the one hand; of generational discontinuity and conflict on the other; and of their simultaneous extension to the central zones of a society as well as to very broad groups and strata alike.

KW: Generation gap

411 Eisikovits, Z. and A. Sagi. 1982. "Moral Development and Discipline Encounter in Delinquent and Nondelinquent Adolescents." *Journal of Youth and Adolescence* 11(3):217-30.

This study compares delinquent and non-delinquent adolescents based on a moral development approach. It focuses on (behavioral) temptation, moral (cognitive) standard, admission related emotions. The authors recommend intervention based on moral approach.

KW: Discipline / Gender differences / Juvenile delinquency / Moral development / Moral judgement / Socialization

412 Erez, E. 1987. "Situational or Planned Crime and the Criminal Career." Pp. 122-33 in *From Boy to Man, from Delinquency to Crime,* edited by M. E. Wolfgang, T. P. Thornberry and R. M. Figlio, Chicago: The University of Chicago Press.

Focuses on offenders who committed their crime impulsively, without planning. Certain attributes of their criminal behavior and careers were noted. Offenders exhibited a greater involvement in crime, coming into conflict with the law more so than their counterparts who planned. Their criminal behavior appeared to be part of a life style that involved readiness to resort to violence and disregard for community conventions about social order or acceptable behavior.

KW: Criminal careers / Planned crime / Situational crime

413 Erlich, M. 1976. "Students' Dissidence in Secondary School Classrooms: A Study of Student-Initiated Conflict." Pp. 79-96 in *Youth Unrest*, edited by S. G. Shoham. Jerusalem: Jerusalem Academic Press.

The study obtained information on the occurrence of student-initiated activity and the conditions pertaining to it. Varieties of initiatives, the circumstances under which they occurred, what purpose they reflected and teachers' reaction to it are the focus of the study.

KW: Classroom / Conflict / Discipline / Students

414 Fishman, G. 1977. "Who Is the Young Adult Offender? - An Adult Who Receives Special Consideration or a Juvenile Who Does Not." *Israel Studies in Criminology* IV:29-40.

KW: Juvenile delinquency / Young adults / Young offenders

415 Fishman, G. 1978. "Youthful Offenders in Israel." *Journal of Social Policy* 7(1):57-72.

KW: Juvenile delinquency / Policy

416 Fishman, G., V. Kraus and H. Lever. 1982. "Factors Affecting Juvenile Court Decisions in Israel: A Multivariate Approach." *Sociological Inquiry* 52(4):292-

305.

KW: Court decisions / Juvenile courts / Juvenile delinquency

417 Fishman, G. and I. Sordo. 1986. "Aging and Delinquent Behavior: The Criminal Act and the Societal Response." *Israel Studies in Criminology* VII:37-53.

Examines criminal behavior of the aged as a symptom to adjustment hardships. The assumption is that problems rose from functioning difficulties in the roles society designated to elderly. Two thirds had no prior records and it was concluded that criminality was a symptom of adjustment to anomie rather than a reaction to a sudden crisis.

KW: Adjustment hardships / Aged / Crime

418 Friedmann, R. R. 1988. "Juvenile Delinquency and Juvenile Justice." *Criminal Justice Review* 13(2):79-84.

This essay reviews five recent books on juvenile delinquency and juvenile justice. The books are: *Children and Criminality*, by R. B. Flowers (1986), *Family and Delinquency*, by L. L. Geismar and K. Wood (1986), *Juvenile Justice in Context*, by A. R. Mahoney (1987), *Rehabilitating Juvenile Justice*, by C. H. Shireman and F. G. Reamer (1986), and *Group Homes for Teenagers*, by A. L. Shostack (1987).

KW: Juvenile courts / Juvenile delinquency / Juvenile justice

419 Friedmann, R. R. 1991. "The Child and Youth Care Worker and the Organization." Pp. 237-54 in *Knowledge Utilization in Residential Child and Youth Care Practice*, edited by J. Beker and Z. Eisikovits. Washington, DC: Child Welfare League of America.

An attempt to utilize the knowledge about organizational theory on structure, process, communication, human resources, rewards, technology, environment and more to provide better service in residential settings.

KW: Direct care / Direct care worker / Organizational theory / Residential settings

420 Friedmann, R. R., Nan Skelton, Mary Jo Richardson, Ruth Ellen Luehr, and Michael Baizerman. 1987. "Changing How Society Views Children." *Children Today* 16(4):10-14.

An attempt to chart youth-oriented policy that views the child as a "whole" and not some parts that need attention. The Minnesota experience with the Whole Child Initiative is described.

KW: Children / Social perception / Educational policy

421 Frishtik, M. 1990. "Physical Violence by Parents Against Children in Jewish History and Jewish Law." *The Jewish Law Annual* 10:79-97.

Points to historical evidence that some Jewish parents have treated their children violently. Examines the attitude adopted by Jewish criminal, civil and family law regarding the punishment of violent parents, the payment of damages to the injured child, and the voiding of the violent parents' guardianship in order to protect the child.

KW: Children / Family violence / Historical research / Judaism

422 Frishtik, M. 1991. "The Sentencing of Young Adult Offenders in Israeli Courts: Probation Versus Imprisonment." *Journal of Criminal Justice* 19(6):525-36.
Examines sentencing patterns of young adults under the Israeli justice system and the extent of use of imprisonment and conditional imprisonment. Legal-penal and organizational models best explained sentencing policy; conflict and rehabilitation models explained least.

KW: Courts / Policy / Prisons / Punishment / Young adults

423 Hassin, Y. 1981. "Raising the Age of Criminal Responsibility in Israel." *Israel Law Review* 16(2):225-49.

KW: Criminal responsibility / Juvenile delinquency / Laws / Probation services

424 Hassin, Y. 1983. "Juvenile Delinquency in Israel 1948-1977: Patterns and Trends." *Research in Law, Deviance and Social Control* 5:25-50.
Describes juvenile delinquency patterns and trends in Israel during 1948 - 1977. Focuses on the scope of the problems through the years, types of offenses, and the relationship between crime and country of origin and offered many graphs and tables.

KW: Ethnic origin / Juvenile delinquency / Statistical data

425 Hassin, Y. 1987. "Jewish and Arab Juvenile Delinquency in Israel: The Problem and Its Remedies." *International Journal of Comparative and Applied Criminal Justice* 11(2):213-30.
Presents the delinquency situation of minors in Israel between 1948 and 1984 and the examination of the ideological basis for treatment models. Compared Arab and Jewish delinquency.

KW: Arabs in Israel / Crime / Historical research / Juvenile delinquency / Treatment methods

426 Hazani, M. 1987. "Prevention of Delinquency Through Repentance: An Ethnographic Study in A Jerusalem Slum." *Small Group Behavior* 18(1):82-98.
Examines a study program developed by a Jerusalem Rabbi to prevent criminality of adolescents who associated with criminals. The study group provided a sense of belonging, cohesion, prestige and rewards and became the reference group for the adolescents.

KW: Delinquency prevention / Group work / Rabbis / Reference groups / Religious repentance

427 Hazani, M. 1990. "To Delinquency and Back: A Longitudinal Study of Very

Young Boys in a Jerusalem Slum." *Small Group Research* 21(4):450-70.

This study provides an anthropological examination of the rehabilitation process of young delinquents in a deprived neighborhood that established a religious study group. The group offered communication, belief, commitment, involvement. The group acted as an effective socialization agent and became a substitute to the youth's background.

KW: Anthropological research / Case study / Correctional rehabilitation / Deprived areas / Group work / Jerusalem / Juvenile delinquency / Longitudinal study / Rabbis / Socialization

428 Heeren, J. and D. Shichor. 1984. "Mass media and Delinquency Prevention: The Case of 'Scared Straight.'" *Deviant Behavior* 5(1-4):375-86. Also published in pp. 762-73 in *Deviant Behavior: Readings in the Sociology of Norm Violations*, edited by C. D. Bryant. New York: Hemipshere.

This study analyzes the possible reasons for the popularity of the "scared straight" television documentary and the Juvenile Awareness Project (JAP). Suggests that factors such as public perception of increasing crime rates, declining support for rehabilitation, and promises of new solutions played a role in the film's success.

KW: Juvenile delinquency / Mass media / Prevention / Shock treatment

429 Horovitz, M. 1963. "The Role of Psychiatry in the Treatment of Delinquency, and Its Possibilities." *The Canadian Journal of Corrections* 5(3):149-55.

KW: Correctional rehabilitation / Psychiatry / Treatment

430 Horovitz, M. 1989. "Who Speaks for Institutionalized Youth?" Pp. 76-80 in *Adolescents in Secure Settings*, edited by R. Roberts. Toronto, Ontario, Canada: Thistletown Foundation.

Discussed the matter of children's rights and particularly of institutionalized children.

KW: Residential institutions

431 Horovitz, M. 1990. "The Juvenile Justice System in Israel." Pp. 105-114 in *The Prevention of Crime and the Treatment of Offenders in Israel*, edited by Y. Tzubery, A Report to the Eighth UN Congress on the Prevention of Crime and the Treatment of Offenders, Havana, August 27 to September 7. Jerusalem: Ministry of Police.

Describes the juvenile justice system in Israel; details the juvenile court, the Israel National Police, the juvenile probation service, the Youth Protection Authority, the Youth Rehabilitation Authority, service for youth and young adults, service for girls in distress, the Arab population's special aspects, legal aid to minors in the juvenile court, child victims of sexual offenses, and the protection of minors from harmful publicity.

KW: Juvenile courts / Juvenile justice / Police

432 Hovav, M. 1965. "Police Treatment of Juvenile Delinquents." Pp. 182-91 in *The Prevention of Crime and the Treatment of Offenders in Israel*, A Report to the Third UN Congress on the Prevention of Crime and the Treatment of Offenders, Stockholm, August 9 to 18, Jerusalem, Israel: Government Printer.

KW: Police / Juvenile delinquency

433 Hovav, M., 1977. *Why Children in Israel Run Away from Home*. Ann Arbor. MI: University Microfilms International.

Focuses on the social characteristics of runaways and their families, the motives of running away and their relative importance as well as their social causes.

KW: Child welfare / Runaways

434 Jaffe, L. 1970. "Child Welfare in Israel." Pp. 331-50 in *Children and Families in Israel: Some Mental Health Perspectives*, edited by A. Jarus, J. Marcus, J. Oren and C. Rapaport, London: Gordon and Breach.

KW: Children / Welfare

435 Kashti, Y. and M. Arieli. 1985. "Social Conditions and Pupils' Responses in Israeli Residential Schools." *Child and Youth Care Services* 7(3-4):51-70.

Describes the structure of boarding schools in Israel and their sub-systems of administration and instruction. The schools are compared to communities representing for the pupils the larger society and a chance to integrate in it.

KW: Boarding schools / Organizational structure / School climate

436 Kaufman, Y. and M. Ron-Menaker. 1970. "The Tel-Mond Follow-Up Research Project." *Israel Studies in Criminology* I:207-40.

KW: Prisons

437 Kohen-Raz, R. 1969. "Some Additional Clinical and Criminological Aspects of Neurotic Delinquency." Pp. 171-81 in *Scripta Hierosolymitana*, Vol. 21, *Studies in Criminology*, edited by I. Drapkin. Jerusalem: The Magnes Press, The Hebrew University.

KW: Juvenile delinquency / Neuroses

438 Krisberg, B., I. Schwartz, G. Fishman, Z. Eisikovits, E. Guttman and K. Joe. 1987. "The Incarceration of Minority Youth." *Crime & Delinquency* 33(2):173-205.

The article discusses the incarceration of minority youth in public juvenile facilities and states that their rate is 3-4 times higher than that of whites. Their numbers were growing despite the overall decline in serious youth crime. The authors argue that it was crucial that public officials begin testing out new strategies to reduce the tragic trend of ever more minority children growing up behind bars.

KW: Adolescents / Minorities / Prisons

439 Landau, S. F. 1975. "Future Time Perspective of Delinquents and Non-delinquents: The Effect of Institutionalization." *Criminal Justice and Behavior* 2(1):22-36.

Examines perception of the future among young prison inmates and young people in other institutional arrangements (soldiers) as compared with other delinquents and non-delinquents who were not in any institution.

KW: Comparative research / Juvenile delinquency / Prisons / Prisoners / Soldiers / Time perspective / University students / Young adults

440 Landau, S. F. 1976. "Delinquency, Institutionalization and Time Orientation." *Journal of Consulting and Clinical Psychology* 44:745-59.

Examines time orientation of delinquents and non-delinquents while controlling for time spent in institutions. Institutionalization was more likely to be associated with orientation towards the present but changed closer to ending term. Emotional reactions were more balanced with non-delinquents.

KW: Comparative research / Emotional reaction / Juvenile delinquency / Prisoners / Soldiers / Time perspective / Total institutions / University students

441 Landau, S. F. 1977. "Temporal Experience and the Criminal." Pp. 129-46 in *Criminology in Perspective: Essays in Honor of Israel Drapkin*, edited by S. F. Landau and L. Sebba. Lexington, MA: Lexington Books.

Focuses on those studies on the dimension of time which are relevant to criminological research and practice. Attempted to analyze the process of institutionalization and to demonstrate the effects of imprisonment on various aspects of the temporal experience of inmates.

KW: Time perception / Crime

442 Landau, S. F. 1978. "Thought Content of Delinquent and Nondelinquent Young Adults: The Effect of Institutionalization." *Criminal Justice and Behavior* 5(3):195-210.

This study reports that delinquent behavior and staying at a boarding facility had an influence on the daily thought processes of delinquents.

KW: Boarding facilities / Experiment / Juvenile delinquency / Intelligence / Prisoners / Prisons / Thought processes / Total institutions

443 Landau, S. F. and G. Nathan. 1983. "Selecting Delinquents for Cautioning in the London Metropolitan Area." *British Journal of Criminology* 23(2):128-49.

KW: Deprived areas / Ethnic origin / Juvenile delinquency / London Police / United Kingdom

444 Muhamed, H. Y., G. Rahav and M. Teichman. 1978. "Ethnic Origin and Social

Control: Jewish and Arab Delinquents in Israel." *International Journal of Intercultural Relations* 2:328-37.

Arab juveniles were over-represented among recipients of severe recommendations and decisions which was mostly due to the harsher recommendations given by Arab probation officers. However, since these officers were Arabs, prejudice could not be an explanation. An attitudes and opinions survey revealed that Arab probation officers were more concerned with the community's welfare than the Jewish ones which may explain the cause of the difference in the pattern of recommendations.

KW: Arabs in Israel / Ethnic origin / Jews / Juvenile delinquency / Social control

445 Rahav, G. 1976. "Family Relations and Delinquency in Israel." *Criminology* 14(2):259-70. Also published as "Family Structure, Family Relations and Delinquency in Israel." *Israel Studies in Criminology* IV:11-28.

Examines the impact of family structure on delinquency. Found that the relationship between family integrity and delinquency was very weak. Also, family relations were not found related to delinquency.

KW: Family / Family relations / Juvenile delinquency

446 Rahav, G. 1977. "Juvenile Delinquency as a Minority Crime." *Adolescence* 12:471-6.

KW: Juvenile delinquency / Minorities

447 Rahav, G. 1980. "Birth Order and Delinquency." *British Journal of Criminology* 20:385-95.

Examines the relationship between birth order and delinquency. There were more delinquents among middle children and among families with larger number of children.

KW: Birth order / Family / Juvenile delinquency

448 Rahav, G. 1980. "Ethnic Origins and the Disposition of Delinquents in Israel." *International Journal of Comparative and Applied Criminal Justice* 4:63-74.

KW: Disposition / Ethnic origin / Juvenile delinquency

449 Rahav, G. 1980. "Models of Delinquency." *International Journal of Group Tensions* 10(1-4):61-72.

Presents four models of the relationships between family relationships, association with delinquents, delinquent attitudes, and delinquent behavior. In a secondary analysis of Hepburn's correlations, multiple regressions showed that none of the models were appropriate without modifications. Smallest Space Analysis was then used as an exploratory technique.

KW: Juvenile delinquency / Models

450 Rahav, G. 1981. "Culture Conflict, Urbanism, and Delinquency." *Criminology* 18(4):523-30.

Describes the relationships between urbanization, social and cultural composition and delinquency in Israel. The low correlation found between the variables was explained by intervening variables such as local youth subculture and having a nucleus of local delinquent group.

KW: Culture / Ethnic origin / Juvenile delinquency / Urbanization

451 Rahav, G. 1981. "Family Size and Delinquency." *Sociology and Social Research* 66:42-51.

The relationships between number of children in a family (family size) and delinquency rate is assumed to be direct and positive. This relationship persisted even when it was controlled for ethnic origin and birth order.

KW: Family size / Juvenile delinquency

452 Rahav, G. 1986. "Delinquency and Certain Structural Characteristics of the Family." *Israel Studies in Criminology* VII:20-36.

KW: Family / Juvenile delinquency

453 Reifen, D. 1965. "Observations on the Juvenile Court in Israel." Pp. 75-105 in *The Prevention of Crime and the Treatment of Offenders in Israel*, A Report to the Third UN Congress on the Prevention of Crime and the Treatment of Offenders, Stockholm, August 9 to 18, Jerusalem, Israel: Government Printer.

KW: Juvenile courts / Juvenile justice

454 Reifen, D. 1969. "Some Aspects Relating to Young Adult Offenders in Israel." Pp. 244-63 in *Scripta Hierosolymitana*, Vol. 21, *Studies in Criminology*, edited by I. Drapkin. Jerusalem: The Magnes Press, The Hebrew University.

KW: Juvenile delinquency / Young offenders

455 Reifen, D. 1970. "Reflections on Child Welfare Laws in Israel." Pp. 183-208 in *Children and Families in Israel: Some Mental Health Perspectives*, edited by A. Jarus, J. Marcus, J. Oren and C. Rapaport, London: Gordon and Breach.

KW: Child welfare / Laws

456 Reifen, D. 1977. "Reflections on Israel's Legislation for Juvenile Offenders." Pp. 189-204 in *Criminology in Perspective: Essays in Honor of Israel Drapkin*, edited by S. F. Landau and L. Sebba. Lexington, MA: Lexington Books.

Deals with legislation until the first Israeli Youth Law of 1971 and various aspects of that legislation, which regulated the adjudication of juvenile offenders. The law introduced new and progressive procedures and methods of treatment. The conservative approach on some issues may indicate the ambivalent attitudes towards juvenile justice.

KW: Juvenile courts / Juvenile delinquency / Juvenile justice / Legislation

457 Reckless, W. C. and S. G. Shoham. 1963. "Norm Containment Theory as Applied to Delinquency and Crime." *Excerpta Criminologica* 3(6):637-45.

KW: Crime / Juvenile delinquency / Norms

458 Rotenberg, M. and I. Nachshon. 1979. "Impulsiveness and Aggression among Israeli Delinquents." *British Journal of Social and Clinical Psychology* 18:59-63.

This is an empirical test of possible differences between impulsiveness and aggression. Impulsiveness is seen as an internal process while aggression was an overt behavior. Delinquents were found to be more impulsive but there was no difference on aggression between them and non-delinquents.

KW: Aggression / Impulsiveness / Juvenile delinquency

459 Schwartz, I. M., G. Fishman, R. R. Hatfield, B. A. Krisberg and Z. Eisikovits. 1987. "Juvenile Detention: The Hidden Closets Revisited." *Justice Quarterly* 4(2):219-35.

The study discusses the extent of juvenile incarceration and decisions that led to it. It argues that in addition to housing juveniles presenting a clear and substantial threat to the community, the new facilities served also as short term commitment options for juvenile court judges.

KW: Juvenile delinquency / Juvenile detention

460 Sebba, L. 1967. "Decision Making in Juvenile Cases - A Comment." *Criminal Law Review* June:347-55.

KW: Decision making / Juvenile courts / Juvenile justice

461 Sebba, L. 1981. *The Rights of the Child in Israel*, Contribution to Goldstein, S. Jerusalem: The Hebrew University of Jerusalem.

KW: Children's rights / Juvenile justice

462 Sebba, L. 1981. "Legalism Versus Welfarism in Israel's Juvenile Justice System." *Israel Law Review* 16(4):461-98.

KW: Juvenile courts / Juvenile justice / Laws / Welfare

463 Sebba, L. 1992. "Juvenile Justice Policy: Mapping the Criteria." Pp. 237-54 in *Ideologies of Children's Rights*, edited by M. D. A. Freeman and P. Veerman. Netherlands: Kluwer Academic Publishers.

This chapter describes the Israeli juvenile justice system's approaches to sentencing on a range of legal-disciplinary to social-helping. The approach decided on was based on age, criminal history and the severity of the offense. Variables discussed were classified into philosophical, criminological, psychological and normative.

KW: Juvenile courts / Juvenile delinquency / Policy / Punishment

464 Sebba, L. and M. Horovitz. 1984. "Israel." Pp. 97-120 in *Western Systems of Juvenile Justice*, edited by M. W. Klein. Beverly Hills: Sage Publications.

KW: Juvenile justice

465 Shapira, R. and E. Etzioni-Halevy. 1976. "The Israeli Student - Activist or Conformist? Pp. 66-78 in *Youth Unrest*, edited by S. G. Shoham. Jerusalem: Jerusalem Academic Press.

Discusses students' attitudes in two areas: the academic and the political. Both deal with the "establishment." Sought to find whether there were signs of unrest in either area.

KW: Political behavior / University students

466 Shaskolsky, E., R. Erez and W. C. Reckless. 1970. "A Cross-Cultural Comparison of Delinquent and Non-Delinquent Boys." *Israel Studies in Criminology* I:98-118.

KW: Comparative research / Juvenile delinquency

467 Shichor, D. 1973. "Some Correlates of Juvenile Delinquency in Israel Development Towns." *Israel Studies in Criminology* II:88-102.

KW: Juvenile delinquency / Development towns

468 Shichor, D. 1978. "Perceived 'Family Attractiveness' among 'Continuing' and 'Non-Continuing' Delinquents in Israel." *Journal of Comparative Family Studies* 9(3):327-34.

Examines Gold's concept of "family attractiveness" as a possible variable in juvenile delinquency. More positive terms were used by those youths who had given up delinquent activities.

KW: Family / Juvenile delinquency / Recidivism

469 Shichor, D. 1978. "Some Effects of the Introduction of a New Correctional Policy on the Social System of Juvenile Offenders." *Juvenile & Family Court Journal* 29(3):29-38.

Examines the impact of changes in the correctional policy of juvenile institutions. The underlying presumption was that changes in the correctional policies would change the organizational climate and would influence the attitudes and perceptions of the juveniles.

KW: Family / Juvenile delinquency / Policy

470 Shichor, D. 1980. "Clients' Views of Juvenile Justice Personnel: Perceptions of Continuing and Noncontinuing Delinquents in Israel." *Criminal Justice Review* 5(2):85-100.

Analyzes the perceptions and the attitudes of the "clients" of the juvenile justice system in Israel towards agency personnel. Generally attitudes were favorable towards probation officers and juvenile court judges but not towards police officers.

KW: Perception / Personnel / Juvenile delinquency

471 Shichor, D. 1980. "Some Issues of Social Policy in the Field of Juvenile Delinquency." Pp. 317-34 in *Critical Issues in Juvenile Delinquency*, edited by D. Shichor and D. H. Kelly. Lexington, MA: D. C. Heath.

Reviews social policies in juvenile delinquency. Indicates the problems involved, suggests viable policies and ways to implement them.

KW: Juvenile delinquency / Policy

472 Shichor, D. 1983. "Historical and Current Trends in American Juvenile Justice." *Juvenile & Family Court Journal* 34(3):61-75.

Reviews trends, dilemmas and quandaries of juvenile justice. Maintains that problems of crime and delinquency control are deeply interwoven with political and social developments.

KW: Juvenile delinquency / Juvenile justice / United States

473 Shichor, D. 1983. "Socialization: The Political Aspects of A Delinquency Explanation." *Sociological Spectrum* 3(1):85-100.

Failure to provide adequate "socialization" is seen as a major factor in delinquent involvement. Some radical Marxist criminologists claimed that the use of the socialization factor as an explanation of juvenile delinquency was functionalist and conservative. A review of explanations for juvenile delinquency in political regimes based on socialist ideology indicated that socialization is employed more often to explain delinquent involvement than in capitalist social structures.

KW: Juvenile delinquency / Politics / Socialization

474 Shichor, D. and M. Amir. 1979. "Some Ethnic Aspects of Official Delinquency in Israel." *California Sociologist* 2(1):69-83.

An analysis of official delinquency statistics in Israel indicated a greater involvement in delinquent behavior of youth from Asian-African origin as compared to European-American origin.

KW: Ethnic origin / Juvenile delinquency / Socioeconomic background / Socioeconomic status

475 Shichor, D. and C. Bartollas. 1990. "Private and Public Juvenile Placements: Is There a Difference?" *Crime & Delinquency* 36(2):286-99.

Examines the patterns of public and private placements in one of the larger probation departments in Southern California. About two thirds of the juveniles sent to institutional placements were placed in a private setting, and one third were assigned to public institutions. This pattern was due to financial arrangements between the state and the county government. There were indications that more juveniles with traditional "delinquent" background were placed in public institutions, while juveniles with individual problems were more likely to be sent to private placements. Policy implications of these patterns are analyzed.

KW: Correctional rehabilitation / Juvenile delinquency

476 Shichor, D. and A. Binder. 1982. "Community Restitution for Juvenile: An Approach and Preliminary Evaluation." *Criminal Justice Review* 7(2):46-50. Also published in *Youth Crime, Social Control and Prevention: Theoretical Perspectives and Policy Implications. Studies from Nine Different Countries*, edited by M. Brusten, J. Graham, N. Herriger and P. Malinowski. International Document and Study Centre for Conflicts of Youth, University of Wuppertal, W. Germany, 1984.

Reviews the major theoretical premises of community restitution programs, concentrating on a description and preliminary evaluation of the Community Restitution Project in Orange County, California.

KW: Juvenile delinquency / Restitution

477 Shichor, D. and D. H. Kelly, eds. 1980. *Critical Issues in Juvenile Delinquency*. Lexington, MA: D. C. Heath.

This book includes 16 chapter on theory, legislation, male and female delinquency, family, education, gangs, dangerous delinquents, juvenile justice, offense patterns, prevention and treatment, developing societies, political implications, and social policy.

KW: Juvenile delinquency

478 Shichor, D. and A. Kirschenbaum. 1977. "Juvenile Delinquency and New Towns: The Case of Israel." Pp. 95-108 in *Youth Crime and Juvenile Justice: International Perspectives*, edited by P. C. Friday and V. L. Stewart. New York: Praeger.

Investigates the connection between socioeconomic factors and the extent and depth of juvenile delinquency in the social setting of Israeli development (new) towns.

KW: Development towns / Juvenile delinquency

479 Shoham, S. G. 1964. "Conflict Situations and Delinquent Solutions." *The Journal of Social Psychology* 64(2):185-215.

Discusses criminological approaches to the explanation of delinquency.

KW: Conflict / Crime causation / Criminological theories / Juvenile delinquency / Stress situations

480 Shoham, S. G. 1966. "Israel." Pp. 115-9 in *Cultural Factors in Delinquency,* edited by T. C. N. Gibbens and R. H. Ahrenfeldt. London: Tavistock.

Discusses delinquency and criminality against a backdrop of social and cultural variables that were identified in the emergence of the new Israeli society. Points to immigration, demographic structure, generational gaps and other variables.

KW: Culture / Juvenile delinquency

481 Shoham, S. G., ed. 1976. *Youth Unrest.* Jerusalem: Jerusalem Academic Press.
This collection of empirical and non-empirical articles on the topic includes and deals with educational confrontation, activism, dissidence, conflict, marginality, intellectual trends, rebellion, counter-culture, subculture, Ghetto youth, protest, deviance, and labels.

KW: Adolescents / Protest / Unrest

482 Shoham, S. G. 1977. "The Differential Pressures Towards Schizophrenia and Delinquency." *Journal of Genetic Psychology* 96:165-210. Also published as Shoham, S. G., L. Weissbrod, R. Markowsky and Y. Stein. 1977. "The Differential Pressures Towards Schizophrenia and Delinquency." Pp. 119-41 in *Youth Crime and Juvenile Justice: International Perspectives*, edited by P. C. Friday and V. L. Stewart. New York: Praeger and in *Israel Studies in Criminology* IV:123-70, 1977.
This study explores whether criminals, autistics, and paranoids could be differentiated from other subjects as for their reaction to family situations on which their fixations depended. It argues that mental illness and criminality were related to a socialization crisis and were not physiological "illnesses."

KW: Juvenile delinquency / Mental illness / Residential settings / Schizophrenia

483 Shoham, S., R. Banitt, R. Feder, E. Segal and J. Smilansky. 1972. "The Etiology of Middle Class Delinquency in Israel." *Human Relations* 24(4):331-47.
This is the third and final stage of the "B'nei-Tovim" project. The main objective of the general project was the study of the nature and extent of middle and upper class delinquency in Israel, the pressures towards delinquent solutions and the preventive policies carried out by the police, the juvenile probation service and the juvenile court.

KW: Culturally advantaged children / Middle class delinquency / Upper class delinquency

484 Shoham, S., S. Ben-David, and J. Smilansky. 1971. "Institutions for Delinquents in Israel." *Abstracts on Criminology and Penology* 2:2-8.

KW: Correctional rehabilitation / Juvenile delinquency / Residential institutions

485 Shoham S., S. Ben-David and J. Smilansky. 1973. "Rehabilitation Treatment in Institutions for Juvenile Delinquents in Israel." *Israel Studies in Criminology* II:230-41.

KW: Correctional rehabilitation / Juvenile delinquency / Residential institutions

486 Shoham, S., R. Erez and W. C. Reckless. 1965. "Value Orientation and Awareness of Differential Opportunity of Delinquent and Non-Delinquent Boys in Israel." *British Journal of Criminology* 5:325-32.

Reports the pre-test replication in Israel of two Likert-type attitude scales constructed in the U.S. to test some major hypotheses as to the formation of delinquent subcultures.

KW: Juvenile delinquency / Opportunity / Values

487 Shoham, S. and M. Hovav. 1964. "'B'nei Tovim' - Middle and Upper Class Delinquency in Israel." *Sociology and Social Research* 43(4):454-68.

Four hypotheses and areas of research as to the etiology of middle and upper class delinquency were formulated for this study: (1) the "masculine-protest," (2) a faulty process of adolescence, (3) the delinquent as consumer, (4) the conflict situations in the socialization process within the family unit.

KW: Culturally advantaged children / Middle class delinquency / Socioeconomic status / Upper class delinquency

488 Shoham, S. and M. Hovav. 1966. "Social Factors, Aspects of Treatment, and Patterns of Criminal Career Among the B'nei Tovim: A Study of Upper- and Middle-Class Juvenile Delinquency in Israel." *Human Relations* 19(1):47-56.

A study of the nature and extent of middle and upper class juvenile delinquency in Israel, the pressures towards delinquent solutions, and the treatment and "prophylactic" policies carried out by the police, the juvenile probation service and the juvenile court.

KW: Criminal careers / Culturally advantaged children / Juvenile delinquency / Middle class delinquency / Socioeconomic status / Upper class delinquency

489 Shoham, S., Rahav. and M. Menaker. 1968. "Institutions for Delinquent Youth in Israel: Evaluation of Treatment and Follow Up, Part I." *Excerpta Criminologica* 8(6):365-74. Also published as Rahav, G. and M. Ron-Menaker. 1970. "Institutions for Delinquent Youth in Israel." *Israel Studies in Criminology* I:177-206.

Contains the primary results of the first follow-up study of the institutions for juvenile delinquents in Israel. Three groups are compared: Jewish delinquent boys and delinquent girls and Arab delinquent boys. Deals with the marginal analysis of the research population, and focuses on the success and failure rates as correlated with various demographic factors of the offenders, their socioeconomic background, family relations and type of offense.

KW: Arabs in Israel / Correctional rehabilitation / Female delinquents / Jews / Juvenile delinquents / Residential institutions / Treatment

490 Shoham, S., E. Segal and G. Rahav. 1975. "Secularization, Deviance and Delinquency Among Israeli Arab Villagers." *Human Relations* 28(7):661-74. Also published in *Israel Studies in Criminology* III:72-85, 1976.

Assesses the level of secularization and normative change of young Arabs exposed to Jewish life and cultural patterns. Secularization and liberalization were accepted when related to economic and technological development but less so when the family was impacted.

KW: Arabs in Israel / Arab villages / Cultural differences / Modernization / Secularization / Social norms

491 Shoham, S. G. and L. Shaskolsky. 1969. "An Analysis of Delinquents and Nondelinquents in Israel: A Cross Cultural Perspective." *Sociology and Social Research* 53(3):333-43.

Argues that patterns of delinquency, in the absence of a well-defined delinquency subculture, may be more maladaptive than structural which could account for the similarity in the responses of the delinquent and non-delinquent boys. Specific explanations congruent with the rapidly changing fabric of Israeli society may have to be sought.

KW: Comparative research / Culture / Juvenile delinquency

492 Shoham, S., N. Shoham and A. Abd-El-Razek. 1966. "Immigration Ethnicity and Ecology as Related to Juvenile Delinquency in Israel." *British Journal of Criminology*. Also published as Shoham, S., N. Shoham and A. Abd-El-Razek. 1970. "Immigration Ethnicity and Ecology as Related to Juvenile Delinquency in Israel." *Israel Studies in Criminology* I:77-97.

Argues that the main problem of culture conflict with respect to crime and immigration rose with the second generation. The process of integration may injure the economic status of the family head and may weaken the cohesion of the family unit and hamper the family's control over the young.

KW: Ethnic origin / Immigration / Juvenile delinquency

493 Silfen, P. 1983. "Youth Prison as an Institute for Rehabilitation." *Medicine and Law* 2:27-37.

An attempt to present concepts regarding planning and organization of a therapeutic program in an institution for juvenile delinquents within a larger prison framework.

KW: Correctional rehabilitation / Juvenile delinquency / Prisons / Treatment methods

494 Teichman, M. 1971. "Ego Defence, Self Concept, and Image of Self Ascribed to Parents by Delinquent Boys." *Perceptual and Motor Skills* 32:819-23.

KW: Ego / Juvenile delinquency / Parents / Self-concept

495 Teichman, M. 1972. "Cognitive Differentiation Between Self Concept and Image of Self Ascribed to Parents in Boys on Verge of Delinquency." *Perceptual and*

Motor Skills 34:573-4.

KW: Cognitive differences / Juvenile delinquency / Parents / Self-concept

496 Teichman, M., H. Glaubman, and M. Garner. 1993. "From Early Adolescence to Middle-Age Adulthood: The Perceived Need for Interpersonal Resources in Four Developmental Stages." Pp. 157-65 in *Resource Theory: Explorations and Applications*, edited by U. G. Foa, J. M. Converse, K. Y. Tornblom and E. B. Foa. New York: Academic Press.

KW: Developmental stages / Interpersonal relations / Interpersonal resources / Psychological needs

497 Weller, L. and A. Tiel. 1976. "Self-Concept and Perception of Parents, Teachers and Friends of First-Time and Recidivist Delinquents." *Israel Studies in Criminology* III:86-96.

This study provides a comparison of first-time delinquents with recidivists as to their self-esteem and attitude towards significant others such as parents, teachers, and friends. First-timers had better relations with parents and teachers while recidivists had closer relations with friends and neighbors.

KW: Juvenile delinquency / Recidivism / Self-concept (self-esteem)

498 Ziv, A. 1976. "Interests and Problems as Possible Explanations of Social Behavior." Pp. 140-7 in *Youth Unrest*, edited by S. G. Shoham. Jerusalem: Jerusalem Academic Press.

This chapter sought to understand youth behavior, and particularly unrest, by focusing on their thinking, interests and problems that bother them.

KW: Interests / Problems / Social behavior / Unrest

11

Law

499 Abel, R. L. 1991. "The Failure of Punishment as Social Control." *Israel Law Review* 25:740-52.

KW: Punishment / Social control

500 Abram, M. B. 1976. "The Criminal Law: Unsuited Means to Achieve Undefined Goals." *Israel Studies in Criminology* III:208-19.

KW: Criminal law

501 Akzin, B. 1967. "The Place of the Constitution in the Modern State." *Israel Law Review* 2:1-17.

KW: Constitution / Modern state

502 Bach, G. 1974. "Development of Criminal Law in Israel During the 25 Years of Its Existence." *Israel Law Review* 9:568-79.

KW: Criminal law / Legislation

503 Baron. A. F. 1974. "The Treatment of Jewish Law in American Decisions." *Israel Law Review* 9:85-96.

KW: American jurisprudence / Court decisions / Jewish law

504 Bazak, J. 1965. "Irresistible Impulse, Diminished Responsibility and Psychiatric Evidence in Israeli Law." Pp. 35-43 in *The Prevention of Crime and the Treatment of Offenders in Israel*, A Report to the Third UN Congress on the Prevention of Crime and the Treatment of Offenders, Stockholm, August 9 to 18, Jerusalem, Israel: Government Printer.

KW: Courts / Evidence / Psychiatry

505 Bazelon, D. L. 1967. "The Relation Between Criminal and Social Justice." *Israel Law Review* 2:35-45.

KW: Criminal justice / Social justice

506 Bedau, H. A. 1991. "How to Argue About the Death Penalty." *Israel Law Review* 25:466-80.

KW: Death penalty

507 Bein, D. 1970. "The Influence of Medical and Biological Progress on Criminal Law." Pp. 196-204 in *Israeli Reports to the Eighth International Congress of Comparative Law*, edited by S. Z. Feller. Jerusalem: Institute for Legislative Research and Comparative Law.

KW: Biology / Criminal law / Medicine

508 Bein, D. 1974. "The Accused's Right of Compensation for Detention Prior to an Acquittal." Pp. 133-42 in *Israeli Reports to the Ninth International Congress of Comparative Law*, edited by I. Englard. Jerusalem: The Harry Sacher Institute for Legislative Research and Comparative Law.

KW: Acquittal / Compensation / Detention / Rights of the accused

509 Bein, D. 1977. "Recent Development in Israel Criminal Law." *Israel Law Review* 12:180-93.

KW: Criminal law / Legal developments

510 Bensinger, G. J. 1982. "The Court System in Israel." *The Decalogue Journal* XXVIII(1):31-4.

Reviews the history of the Israeli court system, its foundations and its structure. Discusses the role of religious courts and other courts such as municipal courts, juvenile courts, labor tribunals, small claims courts and military courts.

KW: Court system

511 Bensinger, G. J. 1984. "A History of Sentencing in Illinois." *North Suburban Bar Association Journal* 1(4)7-10.

Offers a history of sentencing in Illinois, focusing on the development of "definite" sentencing, the origin of parole, indeterminate sentencing, determinate sentencing. These are discussed in the context of increased overcrowding of prisons in Illinois.

KW: Historical research / Sentencing / United States

512 Blum, Y. Z. 1978. "Extradition: A Common Approach to the Control of International Terrorism and Traffic in Narcotic Drugs." *Israel Law Review* 13:194-202.

KW: Drugs / Extradition / International terrorism / Terrorism

513 Blumstein, A. 1991. "Making Sentencing Policy More Rational and More Effective." *Israel Law Review* 25:607-19.

KW: Sentencing policy

514 Cohen, B-Z. and S. Palmor. 1985. "The Impact of Ethnicity on Probation Recommendations and Dispositions in Israel." *Justice Quarterly* 2:197-212.

Examines differences in recommendations and sentencing of Arabs and Jews in Israel. Arab offenders were less likely to receive probation recommendations, probation itself, and were more likely to be sent to prison. Arab probation officers were stricter with Arab offenders.

KW: Arabs in Israel / Arraignment / Discrimination / Ethnic origin / Probation / Sentencing

515 Cohen, B-Z., G. Fishman and J. Soroka. 1985. "Judicial Discretion and Sentencing Disparity in Adult Felony Courts in Israel." *Journal of Criminal Justice* 13(2):99-116.

A study of a set of legal, extra-legal and systemic variables that were expected to influence the operation of the criminal justice system. These variables were used to analyze judges' decisions to seek an investigation prior to verdict and see how such requests influenced the verdicts.

KW: Arraignment / Courts / Judges / Verdict

516 Cohen, H. H. 1965. "Legislation and Judicial Process in the Field of Criminal Law." Pp. 15-34 in *The Prevention of Crime and the Treatment of Offenders in Israel*, A Report to the Third UN Congress on the Prevention of Crime and the Treatment of Offenders, Stockholm, August 9 to 18, Jerusalem, Israel: Government Printer.

KW: Criminal law / Laws / Legislation

517 Cohn, H. H. 1969. "Tortures and Confessions. Historical Sidelights on the Psychology of Law." Pp. 3-27 in *Scripta Hierosolymitana*, Vol. 21, *Studies in Criminology*, edited by I. Drapkin. Jerusalem: The Magnes Press, The Hebrew University.

KW: Confessions / Police interrogations / Psychology of law / Torture

518 Cohn, H. H. 1970. "The Penology of the Talmud." *Israel Law Review* 5:53-74.

KW: Jewish law / Penology / Talmud

519 Cohn, H. H. 1991. "On the Immorality of Punishment." *Israel Law Review* 25:283-301.

KW: Punishment

520 Cohen, S. 1991. "Alternatives to Punishment - the Abolitionist Case." *Israel Law*

Review 25:729-39.

Critiques the abolitionist approach to eliminate penalty that offered alternatives aimed at regulation and controlling law enforcement. Cohen accepts the basic approach but points out some limitations.

KW: Alternatives to punishment / Punishment

521 Dershowitz, A. M. 1989. "Is it Necessary to Apply 'Physical Pressure' to Terrorists - and to Lie About it?" *Israel Law Review* 23:192-200.

KW: Interrogations / Terrorism / Torture

522 Dinstein, Y. 1972. "Criminal Jurisdiction Over Aircraft Hijacking." *Israel Law Review* 7:195-206.

KW: Aircraft hijacking / Crime / Criminal law / Jurisdiction / Punishment

523 Dinstein, Y. 1985. "International Criminal Law." *Israel Law Review* 20:206-42.

KW: International criminal law

524 Drapkin, I. S. 1969. "Criminological Aspects of Sentencing." Pp. 28-52 in *Scripta Hierosolymitana*, Vol. 21, *Studies in Criminology*, edited by I. Drapkin. Jerusalem: The Magnes Press, The Hebrew University.

KW: Criminological theories / Sentencing

525 Elon, M. 1967. "The Source and Nature of Jewish Law and Its Application in the State of Israel - Part I." *Israel Law Review* 2:515-65.

KW: Jewish law

526 Elon, M. 1968. "The Source and Nature of Jewish Law and Its Application in the State of Israel - Part II." *Israel Law Review* 2:88-126.

KW: Jewish law

527 Elon, M. 1968. "The Source and Nature of Jewish Law and Its Application in the State of Israel - Part III." *Israel Law Review* 2:416-57.

KW: Jewish law

528 Elon, M. 1969. "The Source and Nature of Jewish Law and Its Application in the State of Israel - Part IV." *Israel Law Review* 2:80-140.

KW: Jewish law

529 Englard, I. 1968. "The Problem of Jewish Law in a Jewish State." *Israel Law Review* 3:254-78.

KW: Jewish law / Jewish state

530 Englard, I., ed. 1974. *Israeli Reports to the Ninth International Congress of Comparative Law.* Jerusalem: The Harry Sacher Institute for Legislative Research and Comparative Law.

KW: Comparative law

531 Erez, E. 1981. "Thou Shalt Not Execute: Hebrew Law Perspective on Capital Punishment." *Criminology* 19(1):25-43.

Discusses the issue of the death penalty by arguing that it has been extensively discussed but lacked due justice to its meaning and spirit. Thus offered the origins (Bible and Talmud) to add information to this issue.

KW: Death penalty / Hebrew law

532 Feinberg, N. 1968. "The International Protection of Human Rights and the Jewish Question (An Historical Survey)." *Israel Law Review* 3:487-500.

KW: Historical research / Human rights / Jews

533 Feller, S. Z. 1967. "The Classification of Crime in Respect of Continuity." *Israel Law Review* 2:232-69.

KW: Crime classification

534 Feller, S. Z. 1969. "The Forms of Plurality of Offences and Their Punishment." Pp. 53-132 in *Scripta Hierosolymitana*, Vol. 21, *Studies in Criminology*, edited by I. Drapkin. Jerusalem: The Magncs Press, The Hebrew University.

KW: Crime / Offenses / Punishment

535 Feller, S. Z., ed. 1970. *Israeli Reports to the Eighth International Congress of Comparative Law.* Jerusalem: Institute for Legislative Research and Comparative Law.

KW: Comparative law

536 Feller, S. Z. 1972. "Comment on Criminal Jurisdiction Over Aircraft Hijacking." *Israel Law Review* 7:207-13.

KW: Aircraft hijacking / Crime / Criminal law / Jurisdiction / Punishment

537 Feller, S. Z. 1981. "Concurrent Criminal Jurisdiction in the International Sphere." *Israel Law Review* 16:40-74.

KW: Criminal law / Jurisdiction / International criminal law

538 Feller, S. Z. 1989. "Not Actual 'Necessity' but Possible 'Justification'; Not 'Moderate' Pressure, but Either 'Unlimited' or 'None At All.'" *Israel Law*

Review 23:201-15.

KW: Interrogations

539 Földesi, T. 1989. "Reflections on Human Rights: Eastern European Perspective." *Israel Law Review* 23:26-33.

KW: Eastern Europe / Human rights

540 Friedmann, D. 1975. "The Effect of Foreign Law on the Law of Israel: Remnants of the Ottoman Period." *Israel Law Review* 10:192-206.

KW: Criminal law / Foreign law / Law of Israel / Ottoman period

541 Friedmann, D. 1975. "Infusion of the Common Law into the Legal System of Israel." *Israel Law Review* 10:324-77.

KW: Common law / Laws / Legal system

542 Friedmann, D. 1975. "Independent Development of Israeli Law." *Israel Law Review* 10:515-68.

KW: Development of law / Israeli law / Laws

543 Gavison, R. 1990. "Forty Years of Israeli Law: Constitutional Law." *Israel Law Review* 24:431-50.

KW: Constitutional law / Laws / Legal developments

544 Gavison, R. 1991. "Punishment and Theories of Justice: A Comment on Sadurski and Hoekema." *Israel Law Review* 25:351-75.

KW: Justice theories / Punishment

545 Ginossar, S. 1966. "Israel Law: Components and Trends." *Israel Law Review* 1:380-95.

KW: Israeli law / Laws

546 Ginossar, S. 1978. "Outlawing Terrorism." *Israel Law Review* 13:150-9.

KW: Terrorism

547 Goldstein, S., ed. 1978. *Israeli Reports to the Tenth International Congress of Comparative Law*. Jerusalem: Institute for Legislative Research and Comparative Law.

KW: Comparative research

548 Green, L. C. 1966. "An International Lawyer Looks at Comparative Law." *Israel*

Law Review 1:580-92.

KW: Comparative law / Laws

549 Green, L. C. 1975. "Extradition v. Asylum for Aerial Hijackers." *Israel Law Review* 10:207-24.

KW: Aircraft hijacking / Asylum / Crime / Extradition

550 Guberman, S. 1967. "Israel's Supra-Constitution." *Israel Law Review* 2:455-60.

KW: Constitutional law

551 Gur-Arye, M. 1990. "Forty Years of Criminal Law: Development in Case Law re the Requirement of Fault." *Israel Law Review* 24(3-4):560-79.
Attempts to show that in numerous contexts the courts attributed to the requirement of fault a prominent position in criminal law. However, this trend was not uniform, for in other contexts the courts adopted arrangements which repudiated the requirement of fault as a condition for criminal liability.

KW: Case law / Criminal law / Requirement of fault

552 Gur-Arye, M. 1991. "The Justification of Punishment: A Comment on Retribution and Deterrence." *Israel Law Review* 25:452-59.

KW: Deterrence / Punishment / Retribution

553 Guttman, L. and G. Rahav. 1970. "A Two-Dimensional Space for Classifying Legal Offenses." *Israel Studies in Criminology* I:35-76. Also published as Shoham, S., I. Guttman and G. Rahav. 1970. "A Two-Dimensional Space for Classifying Legal Offences." *Journal of Research in Crime and Delinquency* 7(2):219-43.

KW: Classification of offenses / Crime

554 Harnon, E. 1970. "The Right to Counsel." Pp. 239-49 in *Israeli Reports to the Eighth International Congress of Comparative Law*, edited by S. Z. Feller. Jerusalem: Institute for Legislative Research and Comparative Law.

KW: Laws / Right to counsel

555 Harnon, E. 1974. "The Right of Silence in Israel." Pp. 143-58 in *Israeli Reports to the Ninth International Congress of Comparative Law*, edited by I. Englard. Jerusalem: The Harry Sacher Institute for Legislative Research and Comparative Law.

KW: Laws / Right of silence

556 Harnon, E. 1990. "Criminal Procedure and Evidence." *Israel Law Review* 24:592-

621.

Discusses the developments of the Criminal Procedure Ordinance, why witnesses were not sworn in before testifying, prosecution's filing charges for serious felonies without a preliminary inquiry by the judge. Not withstanding the significant changes introduced over the past 40 years, the structure still rested primarily upon common law principles, upon rules established during the mandate period and upon the adversary system.

KW: Criminal procedure / Evidence / Laws

557 Hassin, Y. 1979. "Making Money 'Work' and Post-Verdict Bargaining." *Israel Studies in Criminology* V:205-24.

This study reports that the larger the number of arrests, the greater the prevalence of a criminal subculture that perceived sentencing to prison as paying full dues to society and thus not having to remunerate the victims in any way.

KW: Crime / Prisoners / Sentencing / Social norms

558 Heyd, D. 1991. "Capital Punishment: A Comment." *Israel Law Review* 25:481-7.

KW: Death penalty

559 Kadish, S. H. 1989. "Torture, the State and the Individual." *Israel Law Review* 23:345-56.

KW: Individuals / State / Torture

560 Karp, J. 1990. "An Overview of Recent Crime-Prevention Legislation in Israel." Pp. 7-13 in *The Prevention of Crime and the Treatment of Offenders in Israel*, edited by Y. Tzubery, A Report to the Eighth UN Congress on the Prevention of Crime and the Treatment of Offenders, Havana, August 27 to September 7. Jerusalem: Ministry of Police.

Discusses recent crime-prevention legislation in Israel in the areas of fight against illicit drug trafficking, fight against terror, alternatives to imprisonment, protection of rights of the individual, protection of the rights of minors, and ethical practice of public agencies.

KW: Crime prevention / Laws / Legislation

561 Klein, C. 1971. "A New Era in Israel's Constitutional Law." *Israel Law Review* 6:376-97.

KW: Constitutional Law

562 Kremnitzer, M. 1986. "Interpretation in Criminal Law." *Israel Law Review* 21:358-87.

KW: Criminal law / Legal interpretation

563 Kremnitzer, M. 1989. "The Landau Commission Report - Was The Security Service Subordinated to the Law, or the Law to the "Needs" of the Security Service?" *Israel Law Review* 23:216-79.

KW: Landau Commission Report / Security services

564 Kremnitzer, M. 1990. "Forty Years of Criminal Law - Further Comments." *Israel Law Review* 24:580-91.

Attempts to expand the scope of Gur-Arye's survey on the requirement of fault (same issue, pp. 560-79; see entry # 552). In addition there is reference to the principle of legality, and to legislation in the field of criminal law. Provides directions for future developments and pointed out novel and disturbing trends in the application and implementation of the law.

KW: Criminal law / Historical research

565 Lador-Lederer, J. J. 1974. "A Legal Approach to International Terrorism." *Israel Law Review* 9:194-220.

KW: International terrorism / Laws / Terrorism

566 Layish, A. 1979. "Islam as a Source of Law in the Druse Religious Courts." *Israel Law Review* 14:13-30.

KW: Courts / Druse / Islam / Laws

567 Levy, Y. 1966. "The Treatment of Mentally-Sick Offenders: A Comparative Analysis of Israel Law - Part I." *Israel Law Review* 1:320-51.

KW: Comparative research / Laws / Mental disorders / Treatment

568 Levy, Y. 1966. "The Treatment of Mentally-Sick Offenders: A Comparative Analysis of Israel Law - Part II." *Israel Law Review* 1:421-47.

KW: Comparative research / Laws / Mental disorders / Treatment

569 Levy Y. 1974. "Criminal Responsibility: A Survey of Developments in Israel Legislation and Precedent." *Israel Law Review* 9:580-7.

KW: Criminal responsibility / Legislation / Precedent

570 Libai, D. 1975. "Twenty-Five Years of Criminal Procedure in Israel." *Israel Law Review* 10:225-41.

KW: Criminal law / Criminal procedure

571 Mann, K. 1980. "The Speedy Trial Planning Process." *Harvard Journal of Legislation* 17(1):54-97.

Argues that concrete institutional standards need to be established to give guidance to those entrusted with altering the criminal justice system. Before any conclusions about the Speedy Trial Act of 1974 may be drawn, the author urged for comprehensive analysis of various regional problems under the Act.

KW: Arraignment / Speedy trial

572 Meron, T. 1970. "Israel and the European Extradition System." *Israel Law Review* 5:75-91.

KW: European system / Extradition

573 Moore, M. S. 1989. "Torture and the Balance of Evils." *Israel Law Review* 23:280-344.

KW: Torture

574 Naor, M. 1990. "Procedure and Evidence in Criminal Trials." *Israel Law Review* 24:622-7.

Discusses the issues of right to counsel, testimony of children in sexual offenses, and out-of-court statements of witnesses.

KW: Criminal procedure / Evidence / Laws

575 Nycum, S. H. 1986 "Computer Crime Legislation in the United States." *Israel Law Review* 21:64-89.

KW: Computer crime / Legislation / United States

576 Perelman, C. 1968. "What is Legal Logic?" *Israel Law Review* 21:1-6.

KW: Laws / Legal logic

577 Primorac, I. 1982. "On Capital Punishment." *Israel Law Review* 17:133-50.

KW: Death penalty

578 Potchebutzky, J. 1974. "Is the State Subject to the Rule of Law?" *Israel Law Review* 9:369-412.

KW: Laws / State and law

579 Rahav, G. 1983. "The Deterrent Effect of the Death Penalty: A Cross National Study." *Israel Studies in Criminology* VI:193-204.

KW: Comparative research / Death penalty / Deterrence

580 Ryu, P. K. and H. Silving. 1974. "Misleading Issues in Criminal Law Codification." *Israel Law Review* 9:311-24.

KW: Codification / Criminal law

581 Schmelz, U. O. 1965. "Legislation and Judicial Process in the Field of Criminal Law." Pp. 15-34 in *The Prevention of Crime and the Treatment of Offenders in Israel*, A Report to the Third UN Congress on the Prevention of Crime and the Treatment of Offenders, Stockholm, August 9 to 18, Jerusalem, Israel: Government Printer.

KW: Criminal law / Judicial process / Laws / Legislation

582 Sebba, L. 1968. "The Requirement of Corroboration in Sex Offences." *Israel Law Review* 3(1):67-87. Also published as pp. 183-94 in *Victimology*, edited by I. Drapkin and E. Viano. Lexington, MA: Lexington Books, 1974.

This survey attempts to ascertain the part played by the corroboration rule in Israel and intends to discover the outcomes of the complaints of serious sexual offenses made to the police, and the conviction or acquittal of the accused. It also aimed to note any direct effect of the requirement of corroboration on the various stages of the proceedings, and to examine the type of corroboration which was in issue in the different cases.

KW: Corroboration / Sex offenses

583 Sebba, L. 1968. "Research Proposal on the General Amnesty - 1967." Pp. 16-20 in *Proceedings of the Symposium on Amnesty in Israel*, publication of the Institute of Criminology, 13, Jerusalem, XVI-XIX.

KW: Amnesty

584 Sebba, L. 1969. "Penal Reform and Court Practice: The Case of the Suspended Sentence." Pp. 133-170 in *Scripta Hierosolymitana*, Vol. 21, *Studies in Criminology*, edited by I. Drapkin. Jerusalem: The Magnes Press, The Hebrew University.

Deals with one form of sentence whose very existence in the penal system was controversial: the suspension of execution of sentence and, in particular, the suspension of sentence of imprisonment.

KW: Penal reform / Penology / Suspended sentence

585 Sebba, L. 1970. "Detention Prior to Judgment." Pp. 218-38 in *Israeli Reports to the Eighth International Congress of Comparative Law*, edited by S. Z. Feller. Jerusalem: Institute for Legislative Research and Comparative Law.

KW: Detention / Judgement / Sentencing

586 Sebba, L. 1971. "Minimum Sentences." *Israel Law Review* 6(2):227-39.

KW: Minimum sentence

587 Sebba, L. 1974. "Legislation Replacing Short and Medium Term Custodial Sentences - Israel." Pp. 121-32 in *Israeli Reports to the Ninth International Congress of Comparative Law*, edited by I. Englard. Jerusalem: The Harry Sacher Institute for Legislative Research and Comparative Law.

KW: Custodial sentence / Legislation

588 Sebba, L. 1977. "Clemency in Perspective." Pp. 221-40 in *Criminology in Perspective: Essays in Honor of Israel Drapkin*, edited by S. F. Landau and L. Sebba. Lexington, MA: Lexington Books.

Attempts to answer the question of how it is that a clemency power has existed in some form under almost all recorded legal systems and that no constitution is known which does not provide for such a power.

KW: Clemency

589 Sebba, L. 1977. "The Pardoning Power - A World Survey." *Journal of Criminal Law and Criminology* 68(1):83-121.

KW: Comparative research / Pardon / Survey

590 Sebba, L. 1978. "Judicial Review of the Ben-Zion Pardon." *Israel Law Review* 13(3):417-31.

KW: Judicial review / Pardon

591 Sebba, L. 1978. "Some Explorations in the Scaling of Penalties." *Journal of Research in Crime and Delinquency* 15(2):247-65.

Discusses the quantification of sentencing severity as a neglected area compared with the quantification of crime severity. Shows theoretical and practical relevance to sentencing severity.

KW: Crime / Literature review / Measures / Policy / Research / Sentencing

592 Sebba, L. 1979. "Amnesty - A Quasi-Experiment." *British Journal of Criminology* 19(1):5-30.

KW: Amnesty / Quasi-experiment

593 Sebba, L. 1979. "On the Punishment for Rape." *Abstracts on Criminology and Penology* 19:115-24.

KW: Punishment / Rape

594 Sebba, L. 1980. "Is Mens Rea a Component of Perceived Offence Seriousness?" *Journal of Criminal Law and Criminology* 71(2):124-35.

KW: Mens Rea / Offense seriousness

595 Sebba, L. 1980. "Mitigation of Sentence in Order to Deter?" *Monash University Law Review* 6(4):268-93.

Discusses aspects of "specific" deterrence and "general" deterrence and how the judicial system was interested in achieving both.

KW: Deterrence / Mitigation of sentence / Sentencing

596 Sebba, L. 1980. "The Reparations Agreements: A New Perspective." *Annals of the American Academy of Political and Social Science* 450:202-12.

KW: Reparations

597 Sebba, L. 1981. "A Note on Israel's Law for the Treatment of Drug Offenders." *International Journal of the Addictions* 16:581-4.

KW: Drug law / Drug offenders / Laws

598 Sebba, L. 1982. "On Capital Punishment - A Comment." *Israel Law Review* 17:391-8.

Offers critical comments on the death penalty. Maintains that the public views death penalty as both utilitarian and retributive. Argues that because the possibility of erring in judgment was integral to any judicial system it should not be ignored. Accepts the need to distinguish crimes by their severity, but this did not mean that the scope or type of sentencing should follow.

KW: Death penalty

599 Sebba, L. 1983. "Amnesty and Pardon." Pp. 58-62 in *Encyclopaedia of Crime and Justice*, edited by S. Kadish et al. New York: Free Press.

KW: Amnesty / Pardon

600 Sebba, L. 1983. "The Repeal of the Requirement of Corroboration in Sex Offences." *Israel Law Review* 18:135-49.

KW: Corroboration / Sex offenses

601 Sebba, L. 1984. "Crime Seriousness and Criminal Intent." *Crime & Delinquency* 30(2):227-44.

KW: Crime seriousness / Criminal intent

602 Sebba, L. 1985. Book review of Cain and Kulcsar, eds. "Disputes and the Law." *Israel Law Review* 20:103-6.

KW: Disputes / Laws

603 Sebba, L. 1985. "Policies and Practices of Informal Social Control Outside the Criminal Justice System (Prevention)." *International Annals of Criminology* 23:271-89.

Discusses the issue of social control in the limited sense of restraining deviance and the more larger sense of maintenance of social order or the self-regulation of the social group.

KW: Crime prevention / Criminal justice system / Informal social control

604 Sebba, L. 1991. "Punishment and Its Alternatives: A Comment on 'Non-Punitive Responses to Crime/Punitive Elements in Civil Law.'" *Israel Law Review* 25(3-4):753-8.

KW: Alternatives to punishment / Civil law / Punishment

605 Sebba, L. Book review of M. L. Friedland, ed. 1991. "Sanctions and Rewards in the Legal System." *Israel Law Review* 25(2):266-70.

KW: Legal system / Rewards / Sanctions

606 Sebba, L. and G. Nathan. 1984. "Further Exploration in the Scaling of Penalties." *British Journal of Criminology* 24(3):221-49.

KW: Scaling / Sentencing

607 Shapira, A. 1974. "The Status of Fundamental Individual Rights in the Absence of a Written Constitution." *Israel Law Review* 9:497-511.

KW: Constitution / Individual rights

608 Shapira, A. 1974. "The Protection of Human Rights in Constitutional Law in Israel." Pp. 105-20 in *Israeli Reports to the Ninth International Congress of Comparative Law*, edited by I. Englard. Jerusalem: The Harry Sacher Institute for Legislative Research and Comparative Law.

KW: Constitutional law / Human rights

609 Sheleff (Shaskolsky), L. 1973. "The Innocent Bystander: Socio-Legal Aspects." *Israel Studies in Criminology* II:197-229.

KW: Bystander / Legal aspects / Social aspects of law

610 Shichor, D. and D. R. Ranish. 1980. "President Carter's Vietnam Amnesty: An Analysis of a Public Policy Decision." *Presidential Studies Quarterly* X(3):443-50.

Analyzes the amnesty granted to draft evaders which was, by definition, a public policy decision involving discretion by the Chief Executive. The analysis concerned itself with the nature of draft evasion and military desertion as law violations and the political and social implications of the policy decision to distinguish between evaders and deserters.

KW: Amnesty / Policy / United States / Vietnam

611 Shoham, S. G. 1959. "The Sentencing Policy of Criminal Courts in Israel." *Journal of Criminal Law, Criminology and Police Science* 50(4):327-37.

Argues that the offense and its circumstances, the offender and his background and the attitude of the trial judge had an effect on the sentence. Compared attitudes of individual judges in sentencing.

KW: Courts / Criminal law / Sentencing policy

612 Shoham, S. G. 1963. "Israel." Pp. 184-90 in *The Accused*, edited by J. A. Coutts, London: Stevens and Sons.
Deals with laws and procedures of the Israeli justice system by focusing on its sources. Discusses evidence, legal procedure, regulation about public aspects of trials and more. Makes reference to the origins of Israeli law as anchored in British laws and principles of Talmudic jurisprudence.

KW: Courts / Judaism / Laws

613 Shoham, S. G. 1964. "Suspended Sentences in Israel - An Evaluation of the Prospective Imprisonment." *Crime & Delinquency* 10:74-85.

KW: Imprisonment / Suspended sentence

614 Shoham, S. G. 1966. "Public Safeguards of the Accused in Criminal Trials in Israel." In *The Accused*, edited by J. A. Coutts. London: Stevens.

KW: Accused / Criminal trials / Public safeguards

615 Silving, H. 1969. "Toward a Contemporary Concept of Criminal Justice." *Israel Law Review* 4:479-93.

KW: Contemporary criminal justice / Criminal justice

616 Simha, E. 1990. "Capital Punishment in Israel." Pp. 115-7 in *The Prevention of Crime and the Treatment of Offenders in Israel*, edited by Y. Tzubery, A Report to the Eighth UN Congress on the Prevention of Crime and the Treatment of Offenders, Havana, August 27 to September 7. Jerusalem: Ministry of Police.
Discusses the current laws, the trial, treatment and execution of death sentences and the appeal review and pardon.

KW: Death penalty

617 Zaltzman, N. 1983. "The Israeli Approach to the Evidence Obtained in Violation of the Right to Privacy." *Israel Law Review* 18:215-67.

KW: Evidence / Right to privacy / Violation of rights

12

Law Enforcement

618 Amir, M. 1988. "Police and the Aged Crime Victim." Pp. 133-41 in *Law and Aging: International Variations*, edited by M. L. Levine and S. Bergman. Jerusalem: JDC-Brookdale Institute of Gerontology and Adult Human Development and the International Society of Aging, Law and Ethics.

KW: Aged / Police / Victims of crime

619 Amir, M. and M. Hovav. 1980. "The Israeli Police." *Police Development* 2:1-42.

KW: Police

620 Bensinger, G. J. 1975. "A Class Act: Role-Playing and AV Aids Foster Communications Skills." *Law Enforcement Communications* IV(2):26, 47-8.

Describes the training of law enforcement personnel in communications skills in Cook County where it had been integrated into ongoing pre-service and in-service training programs for criminal justice personnel. Highlights how a communications skills training program has been designed and implemented.

KW: Communications / Law enforcement / Training / United States

621 Bensinger, G. J. 1978. "Metropolitanization: The Metropolitan Toronto Police." *Police Law Quarterly* VIII(4):28-35.

Offers an initial description of the Metropolitan Toronto police to stimulate some thought regarding possible new directions for law enforcement in Cook County, Illinois.

KW: Metropolitan police / Urban policing

622 Bensinger, G. J. 1981. "The Israel Police in Transition: An Organizational Study." *Police Studies* 4(2):3-8.

Discusses the changing crime statistics in Israel where official crime reports indicated a three fold increase in crime and the victimization survey (1979) reported that one in every four Israelis became a victim of crime. This served as a background to a fierce debate in Israel about the existence of organized crime. The article describes the impact of this debate on police organization and how personnel changes, at the commissioner level, transformed the police from openness (under an outsider) to closure (under a new insider replacement) within a period of one year.

KW: Commissioner / Organizations / Organized crime / Police / Police in transition

623 Bensinger, G. J. 1983. "The Israel Police and Terrorism Management." *Journal of Crime and Justice* VI:1-15.

KW: Management / Police / Terrorism

624 Bensinger, G. J. 1984. "Israel Finds Crime Rising, Clearance Rates on the Way Down." *Law Enforcement News* 8(14, November 12):6.

Cites press reports that pointed to a rise in crime and a decrease in clearance rate.

KW: Clearance rate / Crime rate

625 Bensinger, G. J. 1985. "Israel Police Take New Directions." *Criminal Justice International* I(3):1, 6.

Discusses reorganization efforts aimed at improving effectiveness and public image of the force. The tasks for police leadership included restoration of low morale and public confidence in the force as well as improving the human resources of future police recruits.

KW: Planning / Police / Policing policy / Reorganization

626 Bensinger, G. J. 1985. "Israel Police Also Face Problem with Brutality." *Law Enforcement News* XI(10, May 25):4.

Describes incidents of police brutality and reaction to those. States that police leadership appeared to be sensitive to the problem and acknowledged its existence. The author sees that as a first step towards effective policy against police brutality.

KW: Police brutality

627 Bensinger, G. J. 1985. "The Ethical Questions of Operation Greylord." *Law Enforcement News* X(22, December 24):10, 15.

Raises questions about the methods used by the FBI in this operation. Cited a report by the House Judiciary Subcommittee on Civil and Constitutional Rights which highlighted some of the dangers involved in such undercover operations. Recommends the reassessment of two issues: the inadequacies of the present Illinois judicial and attorney discipline mechanisms and the selection of judges.

KW: Courtroom misconduct / Ethics / Sting operation / United States

628 Bensinger, G. J. 1988. "Operation Greylord and Its Aftermath." *International Journal of Comparative and Applied Criminal Justice* 12(1):111-18.

Discusses "Operation Greylord," the largest and most successful investigation into courtroom misconduct in the history of the American judiciary. The target of the federal investigation was the Cook County court system and the success of the investigation is attributed to the fact that it was a typical "sting" operation.

KW: Courtroom misconduct / Sting operation / United States

629 Brewer, J. D., A. Guelke, I. Hume, E. Moxon-Browne, and R. Wilford. 1988. *The Police, Public Order and the State.* New York: St. Martin's Press.

KW: Police / Public order / State

630 Erez, E. 1984. "Self-Defined 'Desert' and Citizens' Assessment of the Police." *Journal of Criminal Law and Criminology* 75(4):1276-99.

KW: Citizens' assessment of police / Police

631 Erez, E. and P. Tontodonato. 1989. "Patterns of Reported Parent-Child Abuse and Police Response." *Journal of Family Violence* 4(2):143-59.

KW: Child abuse / Police

632 Friedmann, R. R. 1986. "Transformation of Roles for Police Officers: Perceptions of a Community Oriented Role." *Police Studies* 9(2):68-77.

Examines the impact of a role change on car patrol officers who were reassigned to community policing through the newly created position of the neighborhood police officer. Transformation was followed by higher scores on occupational prestige and role performance scales.

KW: Field experiment / Neighborhood police officers / Occupational prestige / Police / Police officers / Role perception

633 Friedmann, R. R. 1986. "The Neighborhood Police Officer and Social Service Agencies: A Working Model for Cooperation." *Police Studies* 9(4):175-83.

The study presents a model for cooperation between neighborhood police officers and social workers in social service agencies. The model is unique in that officers focused on "non-criminal" matters and there was a written agreement for cooperation and division of labor between officers and workers, mediated by a university, that included an ethical clause for information exchange.

KW: Inter-agency cooperation / Neighborhood police officers / Police officers / Social work / Welfare services

634 Friedmann, R. R. 1987. "Citizens Attitudes Toward the Police: Results from an Experiment in Community Policing in Israel." *American Journal of Police* VI(1):67-93.

Provides a measure of attitudes of residents towards the police and their community following the introduction of neighborhood police officers

(NPOs) in several experimental neighborhoods. Comparison is made between neighborhoods with NPOs and similar neighborhood without NPOs. Attitudes have increased positively towards the police.

KW: Attitudes / Citizens / Field experimental design / Neighborhood Police Officers / Police

635 Friedmann, R. R. 1990. "Community Policing: Promises and Challenges." *Journal of Contemporary Criminal Justice* 6(2):79-88.

Discusses the theoretical approach to community policing. Questions the validity of relegating crime control to police and proposed focusing on internal police features as well as community characteristics in any attempt to improve crime control.

KW: Community policing / Police

636 Friedmann, R. R. 1992. *Community Policing: Comparative Perspectives and Prospects.* New York: St. Martin's Press; Hemel, Hempstead, England: Harvester-Wheatsheaf Books.

This book offers a comparative study of community policing efforts in Canada, England, Israel and the United States. Analyzes existing programs, discusses the concept of community, offered a definition of community policing, and pointed to future trends as needing to focus on the "super agency" in a concerted effort to fight crime more effectively. Departs from traditional works in the emphasis on the need to curb the motivation for crime and not merely curb criminal behavior.

KW: Attitudes / Canada / Community / Community policing / Comparative research / England / Israel / Police / Super-agency / United States

637 Friedmann, R. R. and M. Sherer. 1984. "The Effects of Different Policing Strategies on Citizens Attitudes Toward the Police and Their Community." *Canadian Police College Journal* 8(1):27-35.

Examines new policing projects such as the sector-officer and police-community relations as compared with traditional policing as to their effect on citizens' attitudes towards the police. Attitudes improved with new projects but so did perception of vulnerability to crime.

KW: Attitudes / Community / Police / Sector officer

638 Geva, R. 1990. "A Progress Report on Developments Since the Seventh United Nations Conference, Milan, 1985." Pp. 14-36 in *The Prevention of Crime and the Treatment of Offenders in Israel*, edited by Y. Tzubery, A Report to the Eighth UN Congress on the Prevention of Crime and the Treatment of Offenders, Havana, August 27 to September 7. Jerusalem: Ministry of Police.

Reports on various crime prevention measures that Israel adopted since the Milan Congress. They included: the National Council for Crime Reduction, the Anti-Drug Authority of Israel, the National Council for Child Welfare, the Prisoner Rehabilitation Authority. In addition, other efforts are reported such as furthering research capacity and development of data bases, combating terrorism, protection against industrial crime, human rights, changes in laws and social control, international cooperation, combating economic and technological crime, legal standards, and international standards.

KW: Crime prevention

639 Geva, R. 1990. "Innovative Methods for Crime Prevention in Israel and International Cooperation as the Means for Furthering These Methods." Pp. 48-55 in *The Prevention of Crime and the Treatment of Offenders in Israel*, edited by Y. Tzubery, A Report to the Eighth UN Congress on the Prevention of Crime and the Treatment of Offenders, Havana, August 27 to September 7. Jerusalem: Ministry of Police.

Discusses Israel's efforts in the areas of legislation for the promotion of crime prevention, the development of an integrated strategy, the founding of umbrella organizations for national activity, the mobilization of the public for voluntary action in crime prevention, and the use of international activity to further crime prevention and control activities.

KW: Crime prevention / International cooperation

640 Geva, R. 1990. "The Founding and Recent Activities of the National Crime Reduction Council in Israel (NCRCI)." Pp. 56-64 in *The Prevention of Crime and the Treatment of Offenders in Israel*, edited by Y. Tzubery, A Report to the Eighth UN Congress on the Prevention of Crime and the Treatment of Offenders, Havana, August 27 to September 7. Jerusalem: Ministry of Police.

Describes some preventive steps taken by the National Council for Crime Reduction (following the shaping of its organizational structure) in the following areas: vehicle related crime, and crimes against the elderly.

KW: Crime prevention / National Council for Crime Reduction

641 Geva, R. 1990. "The Principles of Professional Ethics in Law Enforcement in Israel as Pertaining to the Use of Force." Pp. 80-6 in *The Prevention of Crime and the Treatment of Offenders in Israel*, edited by Y. Tzubery, A Report to the Eighth UN Congress on the Prevention of Crime and the Treatment of Offenders, Havana, August 27 to September 7. Jerusalem: Ministry of Police.

Provides an overview the use of force in Israel, discusses the INP's directives on the use of firearms, and the increased awareness among police and security personnel of human rights issues.

KW: Law enforcement / Professional ethics / Use of force

642 Geva, R. 1991. *Innovation, Exchange: A Bulletin of Innovation and Implementation in Law-Enforcement, Crime Prevention, Incarceration, and Legislation. Issue* 2. Jerusalem: Israel Ministry of Police.

KW: Crime prevention / Law enforcement

643 Geva, R. 1992. *Innovation, Exchange: A Bulletin of Innovation and*

Implementation in Law-Enforcement, Crime Prevention, Incarceration, and Legislation. Issue 3. Jerusalem: Israel Ministry of Police.

KW: Crime prevention / Law enforcement

644 Geva, R. 1993. *Innovation, Exchange: A Bulletin of Innovation and Implementation in Law-Enforcement, Crime Prevention, Incarceration, and Legislation. Issue 4.* Jerusalem: Israel Ministry of Police.

KW: Crime prevention / Law enforcement

645 Gurevitch, M., B. Danet, and G. Schwartz. 1971. "The Image of the Police in Israel." *Law & Society Review* 5(3):367-88. Also published in *Israel Studies in Criminology*, 1973, II:171-96.

KW: Police / Police image / Role perception

646 Hassin, Y. 1981. "Presence of Parents During Interrogation of Their Children." *Juvenile & Family Court Journal* 32(3):33-42. Also indexed in *Inventory of Marriage and Family Literature* (IMFL), edited by David H. Olson. Sage Publications, 1982.

A study of the reactions of minors who were interrogated by police for the first time. Minors displayed fear, shame and regret and attempted to hide their interrogation from parents.

KW: Juvenile delinquency / Parent-child relations / Police interrogations

647 Hoffman, H., N. Salpeter, and G. Novak. 1988. *Survey: Services Given by the Israeli Police Which Are Police Duty by Law.* Jerusalem, Israel: Office of the Chief Scientist, Ministry of Police.

KW: Police / Police services / Survey

648 Hovav, M. and M. Amir. 1979. "Israel Police: History and Analysis." *Police Studies* 2(2):5-31.

Provides a historical, organizational, and social analysis of the Israel Police (IP) and its interrelations with broader social issues. Interest focuses on the democratic political framework, the economic, technological and social development, the repercussion of security problems and the wars Israel had undergone with her neighbors, and the developments in the areas of crime and delinquency.

KW: Historical research / Police

649 Israel National Police. 1993. *Annual Report*. Jerusalem: Israel National Police, Planning and Organization Division.

KW: Crime statistics / Organizational structure / Police

650 Kopel, P. 1965. "Israel Police." Pp. 176-82 in *The Prevention of Crime and the*

Treatment of Offenders in Israel, A Report to the Third UN Congress on the Prevention of Crime and the Treatment of Offenders, Stockholm, August 9 to 18, Jerusalem, Israel: Government Printer.

KW: Crime prevention / Police

651 Landau, S. F. 1978. "Do Legal Variables Predict Police Decisions Regarding the Prosecution of Juvenile Offenders?" *Law and Human Behavior* 2(2):95-105.
his study demonstrates that previous involvement of the juvenile offender predicted the tendency of police to prosecute. Legal variables (such as number of arrests, or crime severity) were found to be weak predictors.

KW: Courts / Juvenile delinquency / Police / Prosecution

652 Landau, S. F. 1981. "Juveniles and the Police: Who Is Charged Immediately and Who Is Referred to the Juvenile Bureau?" *British Journal of Criminology* 21(1):27-46.
Examines police decision making regarding criminals in London during the last quarter of 1978. Legal as well as extra-legal variables played a role in police decision making.

KW: Age differences / Crime / Decision making / Ethnic origin / Gender differences / Juvenile delinquency / Laws / Police / United Kingdom

653 Landau, S. F. 1991. "Police Response to Spousal Violence in Israel: Some Preliminary Findings." Pp. 719-35 in *Victims and Criminal Justice: Legal Protection, Restitution and Support*, Vol. 51, edited by G. Kaiser, H. Kury and H. J. Albrecht. Frieburg, I. Br.: Max-Planck Institute.

KW: Family violence / Police

654 Shane, P. G. 1980. *Police and People: A Comparison of Five Countries.* St. Louis: The C.V. Mosby.

KW: Comparative research / Organizational structure / Police

655 Sherer, M. and R. R. Friedmann. 1983. "Police Preventive Intervention at the Community Level in Israel." *The Police Chief* 50(12):50-51.
Examines possible attitude change that accompanied crime prevention programs offered by police. Fear of crime and vulnerability increased but so did positive attitudes towards the police. Citizens were willing to volunteer more.

KW: Attitude change / Citizen participation / Civil Guard / Crime prevention / Deprived areas / Police

656 Tennenbaum, A. N. 1991. "Police Officers' Need for Self-Defense Causes Brutality." Pp. 100-1 in *Police Brutality: Current Controversies,* edited by W. Dudley. San Diego, CA: Greenhaven Press.
Discusses different aspects of use of force in the work of officers.

KW: Brutality / Police officers / Self defense

657 Yuchtman-Yaar, E. and W. A. Gamson. 1977. "Police and Society in Israel." *Israel Studies in Criminology* IV:67-95. Also published as pp. 195-218 in *Police and Society*, edited by D. H. Bayley, Beverly Hills, CA: Sage.

KW: Police / Social control

13

Organized Crime

658 Amir, M. 1978. "Organized Crime in Israel and the United States." *Crossroads* 1(1):119-41.

Discusses criminality among Jews in the 19th and 20th centuries. Proposes that being a minority in their communities was associated with low crime rates. The author's prognosis is that the situation would worsen as white collar criminal activity would take root more firmly in Israel and diversify by investing profits from illegitimate organized criminal activities to infiltrate and control some legitimate enterprises.

KW: Crime / Europe / Historical research / Jews / Organized crime / United States

659 Amir, M. 1979. "Organized Crime in Israel and the United States. Part II: The Role of Jews in Crime in America." *Crossroads* 2:197-219.

Discusses criminality among Jews in the 19th and 20th centuries. Proposes that being a minority in their communities is associated with low crime rates. In the U.S. Jews, more than any other minority, cooperated with other nationals in the crime world and were characterized as able to break out from local crime to the world syndicate combining crime with legitimate business.

KW: Crime / Europe / Historical research / Jews / Organized crime / United States

660 Amir, M. 1985. "Georgian Jews from the USSR: Problems of Criminality and Adaptation to Israeli Society." *Crossroads* 14:57-77.

Describes criminality patterns among new immigrants from Gruzia (former Soviet Union Republic of Georgia) in Israel against the backdrop of social profile, social and cultural traits and absorption problems. Emphasis is on the traditional way of life, family centeredness and compactness of family ties, attachment to religion, and alienation from life styles and work patterns of contemporary society. Georgian Jews were commonly involved in business practices which, although formally unlawful in the USSR, were in fact tolerated by Soviet society as legitimate.

KW: Acculturation / Criminality / Gruzia / Immigrants

661 Amir, M. 1986. "Organized Crime and Organized Criminality Among Georgian Jews in Israel." Pp. 172-91 in *Organized Crime: A Global Perspective*, edited by R. J. Kelly. Totowa, NJ: Rowman & Littlefield.

KW: Gruzia / Immigrants / Organized crime

662 Bensinger, G. J. 1982. "Organized Crime Israel Style." *The Police Chief* 49(4):42-3, 67.

Describes the rising problem of crime in Israel and police response to it. This in light of Western media reports about the existence of an Israeli Mafia in the United States where they have been linked with crimes ranging from arson and insurance fraud to homicide.

KW: Organized crime / Shimron Commission

14

Political Deviance and Violence

663 Ben-Yehuda, N. 1987. "The Politicization of Deviance: Resisting and Reversing Degradation and Stigmatization." *Deviant Behavior* 8:259-82.

Describes in detail the case of Aharon Abu-Hatzeira. Analysis indicated how he was able to avoid stigmatization, labeling and humiliation by taking advantage of his ethnic origin and religiosity. This was possible due to the ethnic climate and receptive ideology. This is used as a case study to point out that degradation, stigmatization and deviantization can be reversed.

KW: Case study / Labeling / Politicians / White collar crime

664 Ben-Yehuda, N. 1989. "The Social Meaning of Alternative Systems: Some Exploratory Notes." Pp. 152-64 in *The Israeli State and Society: Boundaries and Frontiers*, edited by B. Kimmerling. Albany: State University of New York Press.

Describes the development of alternative systems to provide health, education, economy and law enforcement within Hirschi's crime control theory.

KW: Crime control / Gray education / Health services / Law enforcement / Social services

665 Ben-Yehuda, N. 1989. "Violence Aggression and Conflict Resolution in An Underground Group: The Case of Lehi and Levi." *Violence, Aggression and Terrorism* 3(3):173-90.

Underground movements struggling for political independence experienced processes of crystallization as well as schisms. Often severe struggles which focused on issues of leadership, operations and ideology developed in these groups. As the State of Israel was created in 1948, the Lehi underground movement faced a dilemma whether to be integrated into the new emerging state and its institutions. Against this backdrop the article traces the development of the Levi killing and examined the consequences of the assassination.

KW: Aggression / Assassination / Conflict resolution / Leadership / Lehi / Underground groups / Violence

666 Ben-Yehuda, N. 1989. "Conflict Resolution in an Underground Group: The Shamir-Giladi Clash." *Terrorism* 12(3):199-212.

KW: Conflict resolution / Underground groups

667 Ben-Yehuda, N. 1990. "Gathering Dark Secrets, Hidden and Dirty Information: Some Methodological Notes on Studying Political Assassinations." *Qualitative Sociology* 13(4):345-71.

KW: Political assassination

668 Ben-Yehuda, N. 1992. "Deviantization and Criminalization as Properties of the Social Order." *The Sociological Review* 40(1):73-108.

Deals with crime and deviance as events defined by negotiations between groups holding different moral values. Distinguishes between regular deviance (where power is more latent) and political deviance (where power is manifest). Discusses deviance as weakening the power of the rulers, deviance by those in power, and deviance as a result of cultural clashes. Presents a case of political assassination to illustrate cultural deviance.

KW: Antisocial behavior / Crime / Moral values / Political behavior / White collar crime

669 Ben-Yehuda, N. 1993. *Political Assassinations by Jews: A Rhetorical Device for Justice*. Albany: State University of New York Press.

Reviews political assassinations by Jews from the end of the 19th century to the 1980s. Develops a typology for assassinations and assassination attempts and describes the rhetorical devices used to justify the actions. Details case studies of each attempt based on documents and interviews.

KW: Alternative justice / Case study / Deviance / Historical research / Jews / Political assassination / Typology / Underground groups

670 Ben-Yehuda, N. and S. Einstein. 1984. "Human Garbage and Physical Garbage: A Sociological Case Example of Institutional Violence." *The International Journal of the Addictions* 19(1):1-23.

From 1981 "treatment" was provided to drug addicts by handing out Methadone at the garbage dump at the outskirts of Tel-Aviv. The article reviews the circumstances that brought about this humiliating treatment and coins it "institutional violence."

KW: Drug addiction / Drug rehabilitation / Institutional violence

15

Rape

671 Amir, M. 1967. "Alcohol and Forcible Rape." *British Journal of Addictions* 62:219-32.

Based on known relationships between alcohol and crime against the person (including sex offenses), this study aimed to determine (1) whether there was any relationship between alcohol and forcible rape, (2) whether violence and sexual humiliation were associated with alcohol, and (3) whether there was an association between alcohol and some temporal and spatial factors in the rape events.

KW: Alcohol / Rape

672 Amir, M. 1967. "Forcible Rape." *Federal Probation* 31(1):51-8.

KW: Rape

673 Amir, M. 1967. "Patterns of Forcible Rape." Pp. 60-75 in *Criminal Behavior System*, edited by M. B. Clinard and R. Quinney. New York: Holt, Rinehard and Winston.

KW: Rape

674 Amir, M. 1967. "Victim Precipitated Forcible Rape." *Journal of Criminal Law, Criminology and Police Science* 58(4):493-502.

KW: Rape

675 Amir, M. 1969. "Forcible Rape." Pp. 67-74 in *Deviance: Studies in the Process of Stigmatization and Societal Reaction*, edited by S. Dinitz, R. R. Dynes, and A. C. Clarke. New York: Oxford University Press.

KW: Rape

676 Amir, M. 1971. "Forcible Rape." *Sexual Behavior* 1(8):25-36.

Stated the findings of the Philadelphia study, discusses victim-offender relations and the setting of the crime. In particular, the article focuses on planning the offense, the scene of crime, the modus operandi of the offense, sexual humiliation, group rape, and the aftermath of the rape. The article ends with offering descriptions of the rapist.

KW: Rape / Victim-offender relationship

677 Amir, M. 1971. *Patterns in Forcible Rape.* Chicago: University of Chicago Press.

KW: Rape

678 Amir, M. 1974. "The Rapist." Pp. 169-77 in *Sexual Behavior*, edited by L. Gross. Flushing, NY: Spectrum Publications.

KW: Rape

679 Amir, M. and Y. Berman. 1970. "Chromosomal Deviation and Crime." *Federal Probation* 34(2):55-62.

KW: Deviance / Rape

680 Erez, E. and B. Thompson. 1990. "Rape in Sierra Leone: Conflict Between the Sexes and Conflict of Laws." *International Journal of Comparative and Applied Criminal Justice* 14(2):201-10.

KW: Conflict / Genders / Laws / Rape / Sierra Leone

681 Mackellar, J. S. with M. Amir. 1975. *Rape: The Bait and the Trap: A Balanced, Humane, Up-to-Date Analysis of Its Causes and Control.* Crown Publishers.

The book has four parts. The first part discusses myths and facts about rape; the second part deals with the victim, the offender and the law; the third part deals with group rape, and the last part offers perspectives on why rape occurred, what women can do, and it charts some directions for the future.

KW: Rape

682 Nelson, S. and M. Amir. 1975. "The Hitch-Hike Victim of Rape: A Research Report." Pp. 47-64 in *Victimology: A New Focus, Vol. V, Exploiters and Exploited*, edited by I. Drapkin and E. Viano. Lexington, MA: Lexington Books. Also published as pp. 272-90 in *Forcible Rape: The Crime, The Victim and the Offender*, edited by D. Chappell, R. Geis and G. Geis. New York: Columbia University Press. 1977.

KW: Rape

683 Shoham, S. G. 1982. "The Interdisciplinary Study of Sexual Violence." *Deviant Behavior* 3(3):245-74.

Presents an interdisciplinary model for sexual violence in general and rape in particular. Rape is viewed as an act of a maladjusted person who took by force what he could not get through human relations or love. The rapist had a maladjusted sexual identity as a result of damage during one of the developmental stages.

KW: Interpersonal relations / Models / Personality theories / Rape / Sex offenses / Sexual identity / Sexual violence / Violence

16

Social Stress

684 Breznitz, S., ed. 1983. *Stress in Israel,* New York: Van Nostrand Reinhold Company.

This collection of articles by Israeli authors discusses stress as an opportunity, stress as a social phenomenon, Israel as a stress laboratory, and stress as a way of life.

KW: Criminality / Elementary school age / Psychological stress / Public opinion / Stress situations / Wars

685 Breznitz, S. 1983. "Introduction: The Many Faces of Stress," "The Nobel Challenge of Stress." Pp. xiii-xxi; 265-74 in *Stress in Israel,* edited by S. Breznitz. New York: Van Nostrand Reinhold Company.

KW: Psychological stress / Stress situations

686 Breznitz, S. and Y. Eshel. 1983. "Life Events: Stressful Ordeal or Valuable Experience." Pp. 228-64 in *Stress in Israel,* edited by S. Breznitz. New York: Van Nostrand Reinhold Company.

KW: Life events / Stress situations

687 de Shalit, N. 1970. "Children at War." Pp. 151-82 in *Children and Families in Israel: Some Mental Health Perspectives*, edited by A. Jarus, J. Marcus, J. Oren and C. Rapaport. London: Gordon and Breach.

KW: Children / Wars

688 Eisenstadt, S. N. 1983. "Structure, Interrelations and Solidarity of Elites and Reaction to Stress." Pp. 95-101 in *Stress in Israel,* edited by S. Breznitz. New York: Van Nostrand Reinhold Company.

KW: Elites / Social support / Stress situations

689 Fishman, G. 1983. "On War and Crime." Pp. 165-80 in *Stress in Israel,* edited by S. Breznitz. New York: Van Nostrand Reinhold Company.

KW: Crime / War influences

690 Gal, R. 1983. "Courage Under Stress." Pp. 65-94 in *Stress in Israel,* edited by S. Breznitz. New York: Van Nostrand Reinhold Company.

This study examines individual variables and situations that contributed to valor during combat. The cited soldier was found to be dedicated to his assignment, determined, functioning well under stress and demonstrating leadership, particularly when under attack.

KW: Leadership / Motivation / Personality traits / Soldiers / Stress / Valor

691 Guttman, L. and S. Levy. 1983. "Dynamics of Three Varieties of Morale: The Case of Israel." Pp. 102-14 in *Stress in Israel,* edited by S. Breznitz. New York: Van Nostrand Reinhold Company.

KW: Fear / Stress situations

692 Inbar, M. 1983. "Some Effects of Stress During Grade-School Years." Pp. 181-227 in *Stress in Israel,* edited by S. Breznitz. New York: Van Nostrand Reinhold Company.

Examines the meaning of the 6-11 age group that was highly vulnerable to crises. A smaller percentage from this age group continued in higher education than siblings who immigrated at a younger or older age.

KW: Children / Developmental crises / Elementary school age / Immigrants / Stress

693 Landau, S. F. 1988. "The Relationship Between Objective and Subjective Social Stress Indicators: Some Israeli Findings." *European Sociological Review* 4(3):249-62.

Assesses whether objective social stressors were in fact perceived as such. Found relationships between objective and subjective economic and security stressors.

KW: Coping behavior / Economic conditions / Price index / Social indicators / Stress situations / Unemployment

694 Landau, S. F. 1988. "Violent Crime and Its Relation to Subjective Social Stress Indicators: The Case of Israel." *Aggressive Behavior* 14:337-62.

Examines the relationship between subjective perception of stressors and violent crime rates. Economic, security, political and other concerns were related to murder rates. Concerns were related to theft rates. The higher the national unity, the lower the theft rate.

KW: Crime / Homicide / Social indicators / Stress situations / Violence

695 Landau, S. F. 1989. "The Effect of Objective Social Stress Factors on Subjective Perception of Well-Being and Social Solidarity: The Israeli Case." *Human Relations* 42(6):487-508.

Assesses the influence of economic and security stressors on the subjective perception of welfare and social solidarity. General stress had a positive influence on social solidarity.

KW: Coping behavior / Inflation / Social support / Stress situations / Well-being / Unemployment

696 Landau, S. F. 1990. "Subjective Social Stress Indicators and the Level of Reported Psychopathology: The Case of Israel." *American Journal of Community Psychology 18*(1):19-39.

A test of the relationship between the level of societal psychopathology and the population perception of stress (general dissatisfaction with security, general economic concern) and social support (social solidarity). General stress was positively related to psychiatric characteristics while security stress was inversely related to them.

KW: Mental disorders / Psychiatric hospitals / Psychological stress

697 Landau, S. F. and A. Raveh. 1987. "Stress Factors, Social Support and Violence in Israeli Society: A Quantitative Analysis." *Aggressive Behavior* 13:67-85.

Analyzes violent incidents in Israel during 1950-1981 within a model which explains violence through social stressors and social support. Found a correlation between four social stressors (inflation, income, number of vehicles and population size) and one measure of social support (divorce rate) and violent incidents.

KW: Divorce / Homicide / Inflation / Secondary data analysis / Social support / Stress situations / Unemployment / Violence

698 Lieblich, A. 1983. "Between Strength and Toughness." Pp. 39-64 in *Stress in Israel,* edited by S. Breznitz. New York: Van Nostrand Reinhold Company.

KW: Stress

699 Margalit, C., Y. Wozner and R. Segal. 1986. "Physical Activities in Rehabilitation." Pp. 168-71 in *Stress and Coping in Time of War: Generalizations from the Israeli Experience*, edited by N. A. Milgram. New York: Brunner/Mazel.

Describes the treatment that battle-shocked soldiers received that focused on personal influences, interpersonal influences and reduction of post-traumatic drug treatment.

KW: Battle-shock / Rehabilitative sport / Soldiers

700 Miller, L. 1970. "The Mental Health of Immigrants in Israel." Pp. 55-94 in *Children and Families in Israel: Some Mental Health Perspectives*, edited by A. Jarus, J. Marcus, J. Oren and C. Rapaport, London: Gordon and Breach.

KW: Immigrants / Mental health

701 Moses, R. 1983. "Emotional Response to Stress in Israel: A Psychoanalytic

Perspective." Pp. 114-37 in *Stress in Israel,* edited by S. Breznitz. New York: Van Nostrand Reinhold Company.

KW: Emotional responses / Stress situations

702 Nachshon, I., E. Elaad, and T. Amsel. 1985. "Validity of the Psychological Stress Evaluator: A Field Study." *Journal of Police Science and Administration* 13(4):275-82.

Examines the effectiveness and validity of a psychological stress evaluator (PSE) that utilized voice variables in field conditions. Expert use of PSE results could be valuable for lie detecting in field conditions.

KW: Police interrogations / Psychological stress / Psychophysiology / Test validation

703 Nachshon, I. and B. Feldman. 1980. "Vocal Indices of Psychological Stress: A Validation Study of the Psychological Stress Evaluator." *Journal of Police Science and Administration* 8(1):40-53.

A test of the validity and reliability of a psychological stress evaluator (lie detector through change in voice). Low scores were found.

KW: Psychological stress / Anxiety / Test validation / Crime

704 Nardi, C., Y. Wozner and C. Margalit. 1986. "Behavior Group Treatment." Pp. 142-6 in *Stress and Coping in Time of War: Generalizations from the Israeli Experience*, edited by N. A. Milgram. New York: Brunner/Mazel.

This chapter describes the group treatment approach to soldiers suffering from post-traumatic stress, focusing on two types of disturbances: fears and depressed behavior.

KW: Battle-shock / Group therapy / Rehabilitation / Soldiers

705 Palgi, P. 1970. "The Adaptability and Vulnerability of Types in the Changing Israeli Society." Pp. 97-150 in *Children and Families in Israel: Some Mental Health Perspectives*, edited by A. Jarus, J. Marcus, J. Oren and C. Rapaport. London: Gordon and Breach.

KW: Adaptability / Social change / Vulnerability

706 Raviv, A. and A. Klingman. 1983. "Children Under Stress." Pp. 138-64 in *Stress in Israel,* edited by S. Breznitz. New York: Van Nostrand Reinhold Company.

Themes in the study feature children's stress, the situation in Israel, longitudinal and comparative research on parent's death, anxiety, and professional intervention.

KW: Anxiety / Children / Death / Intervention programs / Psychological stress / Stress situations / War influences

707 Teichman, Y., M. Teichman, M. Morad, and C. Melnick. 1980. "The Motivation Underlying Affiliative Behavior in an Ego-Threat Situation." Pp. 37-48 in

Stress and Anxiety, Vol. 8, edited by C. D. Spielberger and I. Sarason, N. A. Milgram (guest editor). Washington, DC: Hemisphere.

A study of the motivation for socializing preferences. The information quantity determined socializing reaction while accessibility decreased the need to socialize.

KW: Affiliative need / Motivation / Stress situations

708 Wozner, Y. and C. Margalit. 1986. "A Multidimensional Model for Treatment of Post-Traumatic Stress Disorders: Summary Statement." Pp. 172-6 in *Stress and Coping in Time of War: Generalizations from the Israeli Experience*, edited by N. A. Milgram. New York: Brunner/Mazel.

Presents a conceptual model for treatment in a unit that prepares battle-shocked soldiers to re-enter the field. The model focuses on seven areas of symptomatology and had an impact on those suffering from severe post-traumatic stress.

KW: Models / Post-traumatic stress disorder / Rehabilitation / Soldiers

709 Wozner, Y., C. Nardi, C. Margalit and R. Segal. 1986. "Behavior Milieu of the Combat Fitness Retraining Unit." Pp. 136-41 in *Stress and Coping in Time of War: Generalizations from the Israeli Experience*, edited by N. A. Milgram. New York: Brunner/Mazel.

Describes the interpersonal relations in a unit that prepared battle-stressed soldiers to return to the field. Used various rehabilitation principles of treating soldiers as soldiers rather than patients.

KW: Combat stress reaction / Rehabilitation / Soldiers / War influences

710 Yarom, N. 1983. "Facing Death in War." Pp. 3-38 in *Stress in Israel,* edited by S. Breznitz. New York: Van Nostrand Reinhold Company.

KW: Death / Stress / Wars

17

Suicide

711 Fishman, G., A. Moriss-Ditzian and M. Kotler. 1990. "Suicide in the Israeli Army." *Suicide and Lifethreatening Behaviour* 20(3):225-39.

Analyzes the suicide problem in the military, questioning whether military service was a catalyst for suicide or acted as a control mechanism.

KW: Combat units / Military service / Soldiers / Suicide

712 Landau, S. F. and G. Rahav. 1989. "Suicide and Attempted Suicide: Their Relation to Subjective Social Stress Indicators." *Genetic, Social and General Psychology Monographs* 115(3):275-94.

Examines the relationship between objective perceptions of external stressors and suicidal behaviour under a stress model where the likelihood for suicide, and suicide attempt, as a reaction to stress, would increase when public support systems failed or malfunctioned.

KW: Gender differences / Models / Social support / Stress situations / Suicide

713 Rahav, G. and L. Ziv. 1988. "External Restraints and Suicide and Homicide Rates." *Psychological Reports* 62(1):317-8.

Examines Henry and Short's hypothesis that external pressures are followed by aggression against external environment while internal pressures are followed by the person's aggression against him/her self. Level of modernization was found to be correlated with percentage of suicide in the country.

KW: Homicide / Modernization / Social indicators / Suicide / Western countries

714 Sharlin, S. A. and A. Shenhar. 1986. "The Fusion of Pressing-Situation and Releasing-Writing: On Adolescent Suicide Poetry." *Suicide and Lifethreatening Behaviour* 16(3):343-55.

Examines the practicality of poetry written by adolescents as a diagnostic instrument for suicide prediction. Poetry by those who committed suicide was more "loaded" and had reference to "death" and "bad situation."

KW: Adolescents / Behavior prediction / Content analysis / Suicide / Writing

715 Shoham, S. G., Y. Esformes, R. Markovsky, G. Rahav, N. Kaplinsky and B. Wolf. 1980. "Separant and Participant Personality Types of Suicide." *The Irish Jurist* 15:99-110. Also published in *Israel Studies in Criminology* VII:132-47.

This pilot study attempted to offer a new behavioral taxonomy for suicide limiting it to ontological and personality parameters.

KW: Personality traits / Suicide

716 Vigderhous, G. and G. Fishman. 1977. "Socioeconomic Determinants of Female Suicide Rates: A Cross-National Comparison." *International Review of Modern Sociology* 7:199-211.

Examines relationships between socioeconomic status and family wholeness and suicide rates among women. No significant relations other than between divorce rate and suicide were found.

KW: Comparative research / Marital status / Socioeconomic status / Statistical data / Suicide / Western countries / Women

717 Vigderhous, G. and G. Fishman. 1978. "Social Indicators of Marital Instability. U.S.A. 1920-1969." *Social Indicators Research* 5:325-44.

Examines the impact of social variables on marital stability in the United States.

KW: Divorce / Fertility / Marriage / Social indicators / Statistical data / Unemployment / United States

18

Terrorism

718 Amir, M. 1987. "Combatting Terrorism." Pp. 41-57 in *International Terrorism: The Domestic Response*, edited by R. H. Ward and H. S. Smith. Chicago: Office of International Criminal Justice, The University of Illinois at Chicago.

An attempt to describe and explain the response of the Israeli society and government to terrorism. Explains the prerequisite conditions of the formal and informal response to terrorism.

KW: Response to terrorism / Terrorism

719 Amir, M. 1987. "Political Terrorism and 'Common Criminality': Some Preliminary Considerations." *Violence, Aggression and Terrorism* 1(4):371-402.

This study investigates two processes and their consequences: The gangsterization of political terrorism and the politicization of ordinary crime. Discusses types of political terrorist groups in terms of their organization and activities, the counter-forces within terrorist groups that halted the process of gangsterization, and the implications of the criminalization of the terrorist groups on the nature of reactions by various audiences such as ruling regimes, law enforcement and the criminal justice system.

KW: Common criminality / Political terrorism / Terrorism / Typology

720 B'Tselem: The Israeli Information Center for Human Rights in the Occupied Territories. 1990. *Loss of Control: The Temple Mount Events - Preliminary Investigation*. Jerusalem.

An investigation of the Temple Mount disturbances that resulted in authorities opening fire and killing a number of Palestinians.

KW: Enforcement / Occupied territories

721 Bensinger, G. J. 1983. "The Israel Police and Terrorism Management." *Journal of Crime and Justice* 6:1-15.

The article argues that all of Israel's anti-terrorist operations that have commanded the world's attention have been carried out by the Israeli army or other security organizations - not the police. It attempts to attract attention to the efforts of the Israel police in trying to prevent terrorists from organizing and striking civilian targets inside Israel.

KW: Police / Terrorism management / Terrorism

722 Bonn, J. and S. Eran. 1993. *Human Rights Violations in the Occupied Territories During the Sixth Year of the Intifada*. Jerusalem: B'Tselem: The Israeli Information Center for Human Rights in the Occupied Territories.

Describes and documents incidents that the organization considers as constituting violation of human rights in the occupied territories.

KW: Human rights / Intifada / Occupied territories

723 Cohen, S. 1990. "The Intifada in Israel: Portents and Precarious Balance." *Middle East Report* 20(3-4):164-5.

Discusses the effect of the Arab Intifada (uprising) on Israel's Jewish population over the last two years, focusing on the radical and liberal sectors of public opinion.

KW: Intifada / Public opinion

724 Cohen, S. and D. Golan. 1991. *The Interrogation of Palestinians During the Intifada: Ill-Treatment, "Moderate Physical Pressure" or Torture?* Jerusalem: B'Tselem: The Israeli Information Center for Human Rights in the Occupied Territories.

This report deals with the subject of ill-treatment, violence and torture against Palestinians detained for interrogation during the first three years of the Intifada. The report covers allegations about interrogations carried out primarily by agents of Israel's General Security Services in installations controlled either by the police, the Israeli Prison Service or the Army.

KW: Intifada (uprising) / Palestinians / Police interrogations / Torture

725 Cromer, G. 1988. "The Roots of Lawlessness: The Coverage of the Jewish Underground in the Israeli Press." *Terrorism* 11(1):43-52.

Analyzes the way the media treated the Jewish Underground in the months following its discovery. Unlike previous incidents when terrorism was ascribed to the margins of society, the media attempted to remove legitimacy from the terrorists as well as from the "national camp."

KW: Extremism / Jewish underground / Lawlessness / Press

726 Cromer, G. 1989. "The Tip of the Iceberg: An Observation on the Reaction to Kahanism in Israeli Society." *Patterns of Prejudice* 23(2):29-34.

Deals with the relationship between Meir Kahana's political movement and other political parties in Israel. His was part of leaning towards the right wing of Likud supporters as well as religious voters.

KW: Elections - 1984 / Extra-parliamentary movements / Kach (political) movement / National extremism / Political parties

727 Cromer, G. 1992. "In the Mirror of the Past: The Use of History in the Justification of Terrorism." *Journal of Terrorism and Political Violence* 34(2):121-7.

Content analysis of Lehi's propaganda indicated that it was based on historical tales that were given present relevance. Focus was on Jewish heroism but mention was made of other struggles for national liberation. A legitimizing theme for terrorist activities was the sense that only Lehi fighters were the real followers of the past.

KW: Content analysis / Jewish underground / Propaganda

728 Fishman, G. 1974. "Criminological Aspects of International Terrorism: The Dynamics of the Palestinian Movement." Pp. 103-13 in *Crime and Delinquency: Dimensions of Deviance*, edited by M. Riedel and T. P. Thornberry. New York: Praeger.

Following a brief critique of the shortcomings of criminological theories to explain terrorism, the article offers the hypothesis that aggression - in the form of overt violence - was the direct result of frustration. Frustration was perceived as the effect produced by any interference with the attainment of goals, aspirations, or expectations.

KW: International terrorism / Palestinians

729 Geva, R. 1990. "Effective National and International Action Against Terrorism: The Israeli Experience." Pp. 65-79 in *The Prevention of Crime and the Treatment of Offenders in Israel*, edited by Y. Tzubery, A Report to the Eighth UN Congress on the Prevention of Crime and the Treatment of Offenders, Havana, August 27 to September 7. Jerusalem: Ministry of Police.

Discusses Israeli measures against terrorism such as volunteer action by Israel's Civil Guard, legislation, rapid deployment of anti-terrorist forces, development of effective anti-terrorist tools, equipment and techniques, and national and international cooperation in the war against terror.

KW: International action / Terrorism

730 Golan, D. 1989. *The Military Judicial System in the West-Bank*. Jerusalem: B'Tselem: The Israeli Information Center for Human Rights in the Occupied Territories.

Describes the Israeli military administration's legal system.

KW: Military judicial system / Occupied territories

731 Simon, R. J., J. M. Landis and M. Amir. 1989. "Public Support for Civil Liberties in Israel." *Middle East Review* 21(4):2-8.

KW: Civil liberties / Civil rights / Public opinion

732 Yerushalmi, M. 1987. "A 'Control Code' Model of Terrorism." Pp. 77-84 in *International Terrorism: The Domestic Response*, edited by R. H. Ward and H. S. Smith. Chicago: Office of International Criminal Justice, The University of

Illinois at Chicago.

The article offers a discussion of what the West could do to control terrorism or minimize its dangerous consequences. Suggests a "control code" model to limit terrorism and restrain the response to it by defining codes and rules for legitimate acts and legitimate responses. The control code must be accepted by both sides in the conflict.

KW: Arab-Israeli conflict / Terrorism

733 Yerushalmi, M. 1987. "Escalation of Terrorism: The Arab Israeli Conflict." Pp. 135-55 in *International Terrorism: Operational Issues*, edited by R. H. Ward and H. S. Smith. Chicago: Office of International Criminal Justice, The University of Illinois at Chicago.

Describes the sources of the Arab-Israeli conflict and explained the escalation of Palestinian terrorism to a very high level of intensity, sophistication, and media coverage. Discusses the sources of the conflict and the stages of the conflict.

KW: Arab-Israeli conflict / Palestinians / Terrorism

734 Yerushalmi, M. 1989. "A Statistical Analysis of Palestinian Terrorism and Israeli Counter-Terrorism Over Time." *International Journal of Comparative and Applied Criminal Justice* 13(2):95-110.

This is a test of propositions related to the development of the Israeli-Palestinian conflict in the last two decades. It includes statements of five propositions and presents theoretical justifications, evidence to support the propositions, and results. The study found that the extent of Palestinian attacks increased over the years but Israeli attacks remained the same; the number of Palestinian casualties increased over the years and so did the number of Palestinians captured in attacks.

KW: Palestinians / Statistics / Terrorism

19

Traffic Offenses

735 Jacobsen, C. 1985. "The Perceived Seriousness of Traffic Violations in the Presence of a Policeman." *Israel Studies in Criminology* VII:88-97.

Examined the possible impact police officers had on compliance with traffic laws. The presence of an officer (in different traffic situations) made a significant difference only with respect to one offense, that of "not stopping for children at cross-walk."

KW: Compliance (legal) / Experiment / Police officers / Traffic offenses

736 Sherer, M., R. R. Friedmann, A. Rolider and R. Van Houten. 1984. "The Effects of Saturation Enforcement Campaign on Speeding in Haifa, Israel." *Journal of Police Science and Administration* 12(4):425-30.

Examines the impact of signs warning against speeding in 14 streets on the speeding behavior of drivers. A decrease of 64% in speeding, 63% in accidents and 67% in injuries was reported.

KW: Drivers / Haifa / Road accidents / Speed reduction / Traffic offenses

737 Shoham, S. G. 1974. "Punishment and Traffic Offenses." *Traffic Quarterly* XXVIII(1):61-73. Also published in *Israel Studies in Criminology* III:147-61, 1976.

This study provides an assessment of the fear of punishment and actual punishment as deterrents against traffic offenses. No relationship was found, but a repeat offender could be identified by lack of basic driving skills that had to do with personality variables.

KW: Crime prevention / Punishment / Traffic offenses

738 Shoham, S. G., N. Geva, R. Markowski and N. Kaplinsky. 1976. "Internalisation of Norms, Risk Perception and Anxiety as Related to Driving Offenses." *Israel Studies in Criminology* III:162-80. Also published as Shoham, S. G., N. Geva, R. Markowski and N. Kaplinsky. 1976. "Internalisation of Norms, Risk Perception and Anxiety as Related to Driving Offenses." *British Journal of Criminology* 16(2):142-55, 1976.

This second report on the impact of penalty on drivers' behavior in Israel examines traffic norms, internalization of norms, readiness for norm-violation and related anxiety. Anxious drivers were greater risk takers and caused more accidents.

KW: Anxiety / Penalty / Perception / Recidivism / Risk taking / Societal norms / Traffic offenses

739 Shoham, S. G., G. Rahav, J. Blau, N. Kaplinsky, R. Markowski, Y. Shaked, Y. Stein, L. Weissbrod and B. Wolf. 1979. "Reckless and Anxious Drivers: Some Initial Parameters." *Israel Studies in Criminology* V:131-56.

A search for a combination of individual level variables to predict the likelihood of predisposition for traffic offenses and involvement in accidents. The "reckless" and the "anxious" drivers were most predisposed to be involved in traffic offenses and accidents.

KW: Anxiety / Drivers / Personality traits / Traffic offenses / Vehicular accidents

740 Shoham, S. G., G. Rahav, Markowski, F. Chard and I. Baruch. 1984. "'Anxious' and 'Reckless' Drivers." *Deviant Behavior* 5(1):181-91.

KW: Anxiety / Drivers / Personality traits / Traffic offenses

741 Van Houten, R., A. Rolider, P. A. Nau, R. R. Friedman, M. Becker, I. Chaldovsky and M. Scherer. 1985. "Large Scale Reductions in Speeding and Accidents in Canada and Israel: A Behavioral and Ecological Perspective." *Journal of Applied Behavior Analysis* 18(1):87-93.

A test of the efficacy of road signs that provided feedback to drivers, on the percentage of drivers who drove within the speed limit, on the decrease of speeding average, and on accidents. Placing road signs in 14 streets was followed by significant decrease in speeding behavior.

KW: Accident prevention / Behavior change / Canada / Drivers / Experiment / Haifa / Road accidents

20

Victimology

742 Amir, D. and M. Amir. 1979. "Rape Crisis Centers: An Arena for Ideological Conflicts." *Victimology* 4(2):247-57.

KW: Conflict / Crisis centers / Rape / Rehabilitation centers

743 Amir, M. 1972. "The Role of the Victim in Sex Offenses." Pp. 131-67 in *Sexual Behaviors: Social, Clinical, and Legal Aspects,* edited by H. L. P. Resnik and M. E. Wolfgang. Boston: Little Brown.

Reports that one third of the young victims were cooperative victims who knew the offender before the offense. The older the victim was, the more resistance she showed. Some personality differences of victims determined the type of behavior they displayd. There was less resistance to exhibitionism and more to physical molestation.

KW: Role of victim / Sex offenses / Victims of crime

744 Amir, M. 1983. "Jerusalem Elderly Personal Distress Assistance System." *The Police Chief* 50(4):31-5.

KW: Aged / Emergency services / Personal distress assistance

745 Bein, D. 1975. "The Impact of the Victim's Behavior on the Severity of the Offender's Sentence." Pp. 49-66 in *Victimology: A New Focus, Vol. III, Crimes, Victims and Justice*, edited by I. Drapkin and E. Viano. Lexington, MA: Lexington Books.

KW: Sentence severity / Victim's behavior / Victims of crime

746 Ben-David, S. 1986. "The Social Function of the 'Career Victim.'" Pp. 33-43 in *Victimology in Comparative Perspective*, edited by K. Miyazawa, and M. Ohya. Tokyo: Seibundo Publishing Co. Ltd.

This is a test of the hypothesis that the existing rationale, aims, and procedures for compensating victims instead of rehabilitating them and the continued contact with social institutions for victims' services instead of coping independently, resulted in a labeling process and an emergence of a new status, that of a "career victim."

KW: Career victim / Rehabilitation / Victims of crime

747 Ben-David, S. 1988. "The Ethical Issues of the Treatment of Victims." Pp. 157-61 in *Victimology: International Action and Study of Victims,* edited by Z. P. Separovic. Zagreb: University of Zagreb.

The large number of victims in need of help made it necessary, as never before, to look into the situation of the treatment of crime victims and test the applicability of existing ethics to this special situation. Experience indicated that no one of the existing ethics fitted this new field. The author discusses the need for ethics for law enforcement agencies, medical care institutions, victims assistance programs, and insurance companies.

KW: Ethics / Rehabilitation / Treatment / Victims of crime

748 Ben-David, S. and G. F. Kirchhoff, eds. 1992. *International Faces of Victimology*. World Society of Victimology, WSV Publishing House.

KW: Victims of crime

749 Bensinger, G. J. 1986. "Victims Assistance in Illinois: A Case Study." *International Journal of Comparative and Applied Criminal Justice* 10(1):231-8.

Discusses the Illinois Crime Victims Compensation Act, the Violent Crime Victims Assistance Act, the Bill of Rights for Victims and Witnesses of Violent Crime, as well as specific provisions mandated by the state's Penal Code and other legislative acts. Also reviews the victim-related programs of two major criminal justice agencies: the Illinois Attorney General's Office and the Cook County State's Attorney's Office.

KW: United States / Victim-related legislation / Victim-related programs

750 Bienkowska, E. and E. Erez. 1991. "Victims in the Polish Criminal Justice System: Law and Reality." *International Journal of Comparative and Applied Criminal Justice* 15(2):217-25.

KW: Laws / Poland / Victims of crime

751 Cohen, B-Z. 1986. "The Response of the Justice System in Israel to the Rape of Tourists and of Israeli Women." *International Journal of Offender Therapy and Comparative Criminology* 30(3):213-23.

A test of the hypothesis that those who rape tourists receive more severe penalties than those who rape local women. Also examines the relationship between the criminal, the crime and the victim. Those raping tourists were not found to be more severely penalized. Severity of the crime, prior sex offenses, and (being brought from) jail explained 61% of the sentencing variance.

KW: Courts / Justice / Punishment / Rape / Tourism

752 Cohn, Y. 1974. "Crisis Intervention and the Victim of Robbery." Pp. 17-28 in *Victimology: A New Focus, Vol. II, Society's Reaction to Victimization*, edited

by I. Drapkin and E. Viano. Lexington, MA: Lexington Books.

KW: Crisis intervention / Robbery / Thefts / Victims of crime

753 Dadrian, V. N. 1975. "The Common Features of the Armenian and Jewish Cases of Genocide: A Comparative Victimological Perspective." Pp. 99-120 in *Victimology: A New Focus, Vol. IV: Violence and Its Victims*, edited by I. Drapkin and E. Viano. Lexington, MA: Lexington Books.

KW: Armenians / Comparative research / Genocide / Historical research / Holocaust / Jews

754 Decker, D. L., R. M. O'Brien and D. Shichor. 1979. "Patterns of Juvenile Victimization and Urban Structure." Pp. 88-98 in *Perspectives on Victimology, edited by W. H. Parsonage. Beverly Hills, CA: Sage, Sage Research Progress Series in Criminology* 11.

Examines the urban structural characteristics associated with intercity variation in juvenile victimization rates. Points to an unexpected relationship between population density and property crimes without contact.

KW: Juvenile victimization / Urban structure

755 Decker, D. L., D. Shichor and R. M. O'Brien. 1982. *Urban Structure and Victimization*. Lexington, MA: D. C. Heath.

This book includes nine chapters on studying victims of crime, urban structural analysis, victimization surveys, empirical classification, population density, law enforcement manpower, juvenile victimization, the elderly, and social policy implications. It also includes three appendixes on the NCS survey design, definitions of crime in NCS and UCR, and NCS and UCR rates and structural characteristics.

KW: Urban structure / Victimization

756 Drapkin, I. 1975. "The Victim Under the Incas." Pp. 135-47 in *Victimology: A New Focus, Vol. III, Crimes, Victims and Justice*, edited by I. Drapkin and E. Viano. Lexington, MA: Lexington Books.

KW: Comparative research / Historical research / Incas

757 Drapkin, I. 1982. "Victimology: The Jewish and the German People." Pp. 7-9 in *The Victim in International Perspective*, edited by H. J. Schneider. Berlin: Walter de Gruyter.

The author argues that in order to avoid the repeat of the holocaust, to have a better chance to be heard by the governments and the people of the world, the time had come for the establishment of an International Society of Victimology. The author maintains that we have the subject-matter, the scientific methodology, and the experts to develop the discipline as an independent and autonomous unit.

KW: Germany / Jews / Victims of crime

758 Drapkin, I. and E. Viano. 1974. *Victimology*. Lexington, MA: Lexington Books.
The book has five parts: The origin and scope of victimology, the victim-offender relationships, the victim and society, the victim and the administration of justice, and the social reaction to victimization.

KW: Comparative research / Victimology

759 Drapkin, I. and E. Viano. 1974. *Victimology: A New Focus, Vol. I, Theoretical Issues in Victimology*. Lexington, MA: Lexington Books.
This is the first in five volumes of works presented during the First International Symposium on Victimology held in Jerusalem in 1973. This book has two parts: the first deals with the notion of victimology and the second with victim's typology.

KW: Comparative research / Typology / Victimology

760 Drapkin, I. and E. Viano. 1974. *Victimology: A New Focus, Vol. II, Society's Reaction to Victimization*. Lexington, MA: Lexington Books.
This is the second in five volumes of works presented during the First International Symposium on Victimology held in Jerusalem in 1973. This book has two parts: the first deals with the prevention of crime and treatment of victims of crime and the second with compensation and restitution to the crime victim.

KW: Comparative research / Victimology

761 Drapkin, I. and E. Viano. 1975. *Victimology: A New Focus, Vol. III, Crimes, Victims and Justice*. Lexington, MA: Lexington Books.
This is the third in five volumes of works presented during the First International Symposium on Victimology held in Jerusalem in 1973. This book has two parts: the first deals with the victim and the administration of justice and the second with victimization surveys.

KW: Comparative research / Victimology

762 Drapkin, I. and E. Viano. 1975. *Victimology: A New Focus, Vol. IV, Violence and Its Victims*. Lexington, MA: Lexington Books.
This is the fourth in five volumes of works presented during the First International Symposium on Victimology held in Jerusalem in 1973. This book had three parts: the first deals with homicide and suicide, the second with mass violence and genocide, and the third with children's victimization.

KW: Comparative research / Victimology

763 Drapkin, I. and E. Viano. 1975. *Victimology: A New Focus, Vol. V, Exploiters and Exploited*. Lexington, MA: Lexington Books.
This is the fifth in five volumes of works presented during the First International Symposium on Victimology held in Jerusalem in 1973. This book has four parts: the first deals with sex offenses, the second with white collar crime, the third with institutional victimization, and the fourth with

traffic offenses and related victimization.

KW: Comparative research / Victimology

764 Eisikovits Z. C., E. Guttmann, M. Sela-Amit and J. L. Edelson. 1993. "Woman Battering in Israel: The Relative Contribution of Interpersonal Factors." *American Journal of Orthopsychiatry* 63(2): 313-17.

This study examines interpersonal factors in 60 couples who reported violence by male against female partner and in 60 couples who did not. Violent men reported lower partnership quality and less social support than did nonviolent men. Battered women reported lower partnership quality but more positive social support than did women with nonviolent partners. Level of violence was predicted by level of child-rearing conflict and the availability of social support for the violent man.

KW: Battered women / social support / violent males

765 Erez, E. 1990. "Victim Participation in Sentencing: Rhetoric and Reality." *Journal of Criminal Justice* 18(1):19-31.

KW: Courts / Sentencing / Victims of crime

766 Erez, E. 1990. "The Impact of Victimology on Criminal Justice Policy." *Criminal Justice Policy Review* 3(3):236-56.

KW: Justice / Policy / Victims of crime / Victimological theory

767 Erez, E. 1991. "Victim Participation in Sentencing, Sentence Outcome and Victim's Welfare." Pp. 681-701 in *Victims and Criminal Justice: Legal Protection, Restitution and Support*, Vol 51, edited by G. Kaiser, H. Kury and H. J. Albrecht. Frieburg, i. Br.: Max-Planck Institute.

This chapter discusses the need for victim participation in sentencing and legislative responses, it presented arguments concerning victim participation in sentencing, discusses sentence outcome, satisfaction with justice, and victim distress.

KW: Courts / Sentence outcome / Sentencing / Victims of crime / Welfare

768 Erez, E. 1991. "Victims: The 'Eliminated' Persons." *Trends and Issues in Criminal Justice*, Australian Institute of Criminology, No. 33.

Describes the Victim Impact Statement about rights of victims within existing legal principles. The VIS is an organized and structured method of ensuring that the court is aware of important information concerning the effect of crime on the victim.

KW: Victims of crime

769 Erez, E. and E. Bienkowska. 1993. "Victim Participation in Proceedings and Satisfaction with Justice in the Continental Legal Systems: The Case of Poland." *Journal of Criminal Justice* 21:47-60.

KW: Continental legal system / Poland / Proceedings / Victim participation / Victims of crime

770 Erez, E. and P. Tontodonato. 1990. "The Effect of Victim Participation in Sentencing on Sentence Outcome." *Criminology* 28(3):451-74.

KW: Sentence outcome / Victim participation / Victims of crime

771 Erez, E. and P. Tontodonato. 1992. "Victim Participation in Sentencing and Satisfaction with Justice." *Justice Quarterly* 9(3):393-415.

KW: Sentence outcome / Victim participation / Victims of crime

772 Erez, E. and P. Tontodonato. 1992. "Sexual Harassment in the Criminal Justice System." Pp. 227-52 in *The Changing Roles of Women in the Criminal Justice System*, Prospect Heights, IL: Waveland Press.

KW: Criminal justice system / Sexual harassment

773 Fishman, G. 1979. "Patterns of Victimisation and Notification." *British Journal of Criminology* 19(2):146-57.

This study reports that victims were not vulnerable to all crimes. Residential areas may had some impact on the likelihood of someone to become a victim. Lower income areas were more likely to result in greater vulnerability to physical violence. Low reporting of crime was associated with higher income areas and property crimes.

KW: Crime / Haifa / Residence / Victims of Crime

774 Fishman, G. 1984. "Differential Victimization Rates, a Victimization Study in Differential Residential Areas in Haifa." Pp. 45-9 in *Victimization and Fear of Crime, Cross National Perspectives,* edited by R. Block. U.S. Department of Justice, August.

KW: Haifa / Residence / Police / Victimization rate / Victims of crime

775 Fishman, G. and G. Weimann. 1985. "Presenting the Victim: Sex-Based Bias in Press Reports on Crime." *Justice Quarterly* 2(4):491-503.

Deals with media images and social reality in a relatively neglected area - female criminality and the perception of the female offender. Presumably, the media's portrayal of female offenders represented to a large extent the existing social attitudes towards female criminality.

KW: Sex-based bias / Press / Victims of crime

776 Frishtik, M. 1989. "Physical and Sexual Violence by Husbands as a Reason for Imposing a Divorce in Jewish Law." *The Jewish Law Annual* 9:145-69.

Examines whether real physical violence against wives was sufficient cause to force the husband to get a divorce according to Jewish law. In serious cases rabbinical court would force a divorce, but not so in less serious cases. This is based on review of rabbinical decisions, but it requires further empirical validation.

KW: Battered women / Divorce / Family violence / Judaism / Laws / Marital relations / Rabbis / Sexual abuse

777 Frishtik, M. 1990. "Violence Against Women in Judaism." *Journal of Psychology and Judaism* 14(3):131-53.

Deals with violence of husbands against their wives in the Jewish society since the biblical period. According to the literature review, there was reference to behavior that included physical and emotional abuse, sexual violence and even murder. Most rabbinical sources displayed attitudes of abhorrence towards the phenomenon.

KW: Family violence / Historical research / Judaism / Marital relations / Women

778 Goldstein, N. 1974. "Reparation by the Offender to the Victim as a Method of Rehabilitation for Both." Pp. 193-207 in *Victimology: A New Focus, Vol. II, Society's Reaction to Victimization*, edited by I. Drapkin and E. Viano. Lexington, MA: Lexington Books.

KW: Rehabilitation / Reparations / Victims of crime

779 Harlap, S. and I. Drapkin. 1975. "Child Injury in West Jerusalem." Pp. 165-76 in *Victimology: A New Focus, Vol. IV: Violence and Its Victims*, edited by I. Drapkin and E. Viano. Lexington, MA: Lexington Books.

KW: Child abuse / Child injury / Jerusalem

780 Hassin, Y. 1984. "Victimization of Households in Israel." *Victimology* 9(3-4):353-63. Also published as pp. 218-31 in *Victimology in Comparative Perspective*, edited by K. Miyazawa and M. Ohya. Tokyo: Seibundo Publishing Co., Ltd., 1986.

Sought to find out the rate of victimization for property offenses and vehicle theft. The study also sought to identify the effect of socio-demographic variables of heads of households and their vulnerability to crime. No such relationship was found.

KW: Complaints / Thefts / Victims of crime

781 Hasson, U. and L. Sebba. 1974. "Compensation to Victims of Crime: A Comparative Survey." Pp. 103-120 in *Victimology: A New Focus, Vol. II, Society's Reaction to Victimization*, edited by I. Drapkin and E. Viano. Lexington, MA: Lexington Books.

KW: Comparative research / Compensation / Survey / Victims of crime

782 Horovitz, M. 1963. "The Psychotherapy of Infanticide - Supplementary Remarks." *The Israel Annals of Psychiatry and Related Disciplines* 1(2):306-10.

KW: Children / Homicide / Infanticide / Psychotherapy

783 Horovitz, M. 1966. "A Survey on Procurers in Israel, 1961-1963." *The Israel Annals of Psychiatry and Related Disciplines* 4(2):219-27.

KW: Procurers / Survey

784 Horovitz, M. and H. Winnik. 1961. "The Problem of Infanticide." *The British Journal of Criminology* 2:40-52.

KW: Children / Homicide / Infanticide

785 Horowitz, M. and M. Amir. 1975. "The Probation Officer, the Offender and the Victim of the Criminal Offense." Pp. 95-106 in *Victimology: A New Focus, Vol. III, Crimes, Victims and Justice*, edited by I. Drapkin and E. Viano. Lexington, MA: Lexington Books.

KW: Criminal offense / Offender / Probation officers / Victims of crime

786 Jacobsen, C. 1975. "Condoned Mass Deviance and Its Victims: A Preliminary Statement." Pp. 91-8 in *Victimology: A New Focus, Vol. IV: Violence and Its Victims*, edited by I. Drapkin and E. Viano. Lexington, MA: Lexington Books.

KW: Mass deviance / Victims of crime

787 Landau, S. F. 1974. "The Offender's Perception of the Victim." Pp. 137-54 in *Victimology: A New Focus, Vol. I, Theoretical Issues in Victimology*, edited by I. Drapkin and E. Viano. Lexington, MA: Lexington Books.

KW: Offender / Perception of victim / Victims of crime

788 Landau, S. F., I. Drapkin, and S. Arad. 1974. "Homicide Victims and Offenders: An Israeli Study." *Journal of Criminal Law and Criminology* 65(3):390-6. Also published as pp. 87-93 in *The Aldine Crime and Justice Annual*, edited by S. L. Halleck et al. Chicago: Aldine Publishing Co., 1975.

KW: Homicide / Offender

789 Landau, S. F. and R. E. Freeman-Longo. 1990. "Classifying Victims: A Proposed Multidimensional Victimological Typology." *International Review of Victimology* 1(3):267-86.

Offers a multi-dimensional typology for victimological classification with the following 11 dimensions: source of victimization, legal framework, offender's intention, victim's identification, victim's vulnerability, victim's perception of victimization, others' perception of victimization, victimization type, severity of victimization, victim-offender relationship, victim's contribution to event.

KW: Classifying victims / Typology / Victims of crime

790 Landau, S. F. and L. Sebba. 1991. "Victimological Research in Israel: Past and Current Perspectives." Pp. 179-205 in *Victims and Criminal Justice, Victimological Research: Stocktaking and Prospects*, Vol 50, edited by G. Kaiser, H. Kury and H. J. Albrecht. Frieburg, i. Br.: Max-Planck Institute.

Reviews and analyzes victimological research in Israel in the last 15 years. Starts with review of victimological surveys, research on children victims, women victims, elderly victims, terror victims and holocaust victims. Also discusses socio-political conflicts that create minority victims in Israel.

KW: Child abuse / Literature review / Sex offenses / Social disputes / Victims of crime

791 Lowenstein, A. 1989. "The Elderly Victim and the Welfare Services." Pp. 99-110 in *Stress, Conflict and Abuse of the Elderly*, edited by R. S. Wolf and S. Bergman. Jerusalem: Brookdale Institute.

A study of social policies and the reaction of welfare services to elderly persons who fell victim to crime and violence. Fear of crime was found to be stronger than crime itself, and it impacted elderly worse than it did younger persons.

KW: Aged / Social policy / Victims of crime / Violence / Welfare services

792 Mendelsohn, B. 1963. "The Origin of the Doctrine of Victimology." *Excerpta Criminologica* 3(3):239-44. Also published as pp. 3-12 in *Victimology*, edited by I. Drapkin and E. Viano. Lexington, MA: Lexington Books, 1974.

Profiles the accused focusing on the personality of the offender (biological, psychological and social backgrounds) as well as that of the victim and the relationships between them. Discusses biological and psychological grounds for fear and intimidation.

KW: Rape / Victims of crime / Victimology

793 Mendelsohn, B. 1974. "Victimology and the Technical and Social Sciences: A Call for the Establishment of Victimology Clinics." Pp. 25-36 in *Victimology: A New Focus, Vol. I, Theoretical Issues in Victimology,* edited by I. Drapkin and E. Viano. Lexington, MA: Lexington Books.

KW: Rehabilitation / Social sciences / Technical sciences / Victims of crime / Victimology clinics

794 Mendelsohn, B. 1982. "Socio-Analytic Introduction to Research in a General Victimological and Criminological Perspective." Pp. 59-64 in *The Victim in International Perspective*, edited by H. J. Schneider. Berlin: Walter de Gruyter.

Offers a discussion of "victimity" as various traits common to all categories of victims who suffered some damage with social implications, and of victimology, defined as that branch of science which is concerned with all socially relevant categories of victims, individual and collective, with regard to the different types of damage.

KW: Criminological theories / Victimity / Victimology / Victims of crime

795 Meyersohn, J. 1974. "Pre-Existing Pathological Changes in Accident Victims and the Issue of Compensation." Pp. 227-30 in *Victimology: A New Focus, Vol. II, Society's Reaction to Victimization*, edited by I. Drapkin and E. Viano. Lexington, MA: Lexington Books.

KW: Accidents / Compensation / Pathology / Victims of crime

796 Miller, A. L. and L. Sebba. 1987. "Crime Victim Compensation: An Israeli Proposal." *The Comparative and International Law Journal of Southern Africa* 20(1):47-78.

Discusses the plight of crime victims and offers a plan for compensation by both offender and the state.

KW: Comparative research / Compensation / Policy / Victims of crime

797 O'Brien, R. M., D. Shichor and D. L. Decker. 1982-83. "Urban Structure and Household Victimization of the Elderly." *International Journal of Aging and Human Development* 15(1):41-9.

Studies household victimization rates as they were determined by the United States Census Bureau. Intercity variation in two types of household victimization was highly related to population density and socioeconomic conditions

KW: Aged / Urban areas / Victims of crime

798 Ranish, D. R. and D. Shichor. 1985. "The Victim's Role in the Penal Process: Recent Developments in California." *Federal Probation* XLIX(1):50-7.

Examines the procedures instituted in California which allowed a victim or victim's next of kin to appear at a sentencing hearing or a parole board panel to state their opposition regarding the crime, the criminal, and the possible options that should be considered for the offender.

KW: Penal process / Victimization

799 Rattner, A. and G. Fishman. 1989. "Wrongfully Convicted - A New Type of Victim?" Pp. 235-48 in *Victimology: International Action and Study of Victims*, Vol. II, edited by Z. P. Separovic. Zagreb: University of Zagreb.

KW: Courts / Justice / Wrongful conviction

800 Reifen, D. 1975. "Court Procedures in Israel to Protect Child-Victims of Sexual Assaults." Pp. 67-72 in *Victimology: A New Focus, Vol. III, Crimes, Victims and Justice*, edited by I. Drapkin and E. Viano. Lexington, MA: Lexington Books.

KW: Courts / Sexual abuse / Victims of crime

801 Sebba, L. 1982. "The Victim's Role in the Penal Process - The Need for a Theoretical Orientation." *American Journal of Comparative Law* 30:217-40.

KW: Sentencing / Victim's role / Victims of crime

802 Sebba, L. 1982. "Victimological Aspects of the German Reparations Agreements with the Jewish People." Pp. 381-90 in *The Victim in International Perspective*, edited by H. J. Schneider. Berlin: Walter de Gruyter.

Discusses (1) the history, content and dimensions of the reparations agreements, (2) the fundamental moral dilemmas involved, (3) some specific issues resulting from the special circumstances of the agreement, and (4) the relationship of the holocaust and reparations issues to victimology in general.

KW: Germany / Jews / Reparations / Victims of crime

803 Sebba, L. 1986. "Victims of Offences." Pp. 377-92 in *Criminal Law in Action: An Overview of Current Issues in Western Societies*, edited by J. Van Dijk, C. Haffmans, F. Rüter, J. Schutte and S. Stolwijk. Gouda Quint: Arnhem.

By examining the role of the victim the article provides a basis for an examination of the relationship between criminal law and (1) civil law, (2) welfare law, and (3) the behavioral sciences.

KW: Victims of crime

804 Sebba, L. 1989. "Victims and the Parameters of a Justice System." Pp. 13-24 in *Victimology: International Action and Study of Victims*, Vol. II, edited by Z. P. Separovic. Zagreb: University of Zagreb.

KW: Criminal justice system / Victims of crime

805 Sebba, L. and S. Cahan. 1975. "Sex Offenses: The Genuine and the Doubted Victim." Pp. 29-46 in *Victimology: A New Focus, Vol. V, Exploiters and Exploited*, edited by I. Drapkin and E. Viano. Lexington, MA: Lexington Books.

KW: Sex offenses / Victims of crime

806 Sheleff (Shaskolski), L. 1974. "The Criminal Triad: Bystander, Victim and Criminal." Pp. 111-26 in *Victimology: A New Focus, Vol. I, Theoretical Issues in Victimology*, edited by I. Drapkin and E. Viano. Lexington, MA: Lexington Books.

KW: Bystander / Criminals / Victims of crime

807 Sheleff-Shaskolsky, L. and D. Shichor 1980. "Victimological Aspects of Bystander Involvement." *Crime & Delinquency* 26(2):193-201.

Suggests that concepts derived from victimology may be useful in analyzing the role of the bystander who witnessed a criminal offense. The bystander may be perceived as harmed by the direct effect of the offense, by the psychological consequences and by involvement in the criminal process.

KW: Bystander / Victims of crime

808 Shichor, D. 1975. "The Wrongfully Accused and the Criminal Justice System." Pp. 121-34 in *Victimology: A New Focus, Vol. III, Crimes, Victims and Justice*, edited by I. Drapkin and E. Viano. Lexington, MA: Lexington Books.

KW: Courts / Justice / Wrongfully accused

809 Shichor, D. 1987. "The Ramifications of Victim Dissatisfaction with the Criminal Justice System." *Prosecutor's Brief* X(4):24-7.

Analyzes reasons for victim dissatisfaction with the criminal justice system and suggested some possible ways of remedying the situation.

KW: Dissatisfaction / Victimization

810 Shichor, D. 1989. "Corporate Deviance and Corporate Victimization: A Review and Some Elaborations." *International Review of Victimology* 1(1):67-88.

A review of the literature is used to analyze various classifications of corporate violations, harms, victimizations and victims. Multiple victims were found with indirect and direct victimization and with widescale inter-organizational victimization.

KW: Corporate deviance / Corporate victimization

811 Shichor, D., D. L. Decker and R. M. O'Brien. 1979. "Population Density and Criminal Victimization: Some Unexpected Findings in Central Cities." *Criminology* 17(2):184-93.

This analysis of National Crime Survey victimization data collected by the Census Bureau in 16 large American cities for 1974 reveals no simple relationship between population density and crime rate.

KW: Population density / Urban areas / Victims of crime

812 Shichor, D., D. L. Decker and R. M. O'Brien. 1980. "The Relationship of Criminal Victimization, Police Per Capita and Population Density in Twenty-Six Cities." *Journal of Criminal Justice* 8(5):309-16.

Examines the relationship between indicators of environmental control and criminal victimization rates. Using a typology of criminal victimization that classified crime as property crimes with contact, property crimes without contact, and nonproperty assaultive crimes, it was found that both the number of police per capita and population density were negatively related to property crimes without contact and nonproperty assaultive crimes. However, the number of police per capita was not related to property crimes with contact, while population density was positively related to these crimes.

KW: Population density / Victimization

813 Shoham, S. G. 1988. "Valhalla, Calvary and Auschwitz." *Jerusalem Quarterly* 35:87-100. Also published as pp. 55-66 in *Victimology: International Action and Study of Victims,* edited by Z. P. Separovic. Zagreb: University of Zagreb.

Offers a theoretical approach to explain the causes for Nazi behavior during the holocaust. Discusses the basic dialectic of the German and Jewish social character. Social, religious, mythical, historical and family differences between the two groups created a long-lived stigmatization that was epitomized in Auschwitz.

KW: Germany / Holocaust / Jews

814 Silfen, P. 1986. "Victimology Without a Victim." Pp. 189-94 in *Psychiatry, Law and Ethics*, edited by A. Carmi, S. Schneider, A. Hefez. New York: Springer-Verlag.

KW: Victims of crime / Victimology

21

White Collar Crime

815 Amir, M. "Computer Embezzlement: Prevention and Control." *The Computer Bulletin* 15(1):397-401.

KW: Computer crime / Embezzlement / White collar crime

816 Ben-David, S. 1991. "Personality Traits in White-Collar Offenders." *Medicine and Law* 10:527-36.

Compares personality traits found in white-collar offenders in relation to the general public and the criminal population, particularly property and sex offenders who made up the majority of convicted prisoners.

KW: Offender / Personality traits / White collar crime

817 Cromer, G. 1982. "The Yadlin Affair: The Anatomy of a Scoop." Pp. 319-26 in *The Victim in International Perspective*, edited by H. J. Schneider. Berlin: Walter de Gruyter.

The article attempts to analyze various aspects of the controversy surrounding the Yadlin Affair (corruption charges against Yadlin were brought when he was nominated as the governor of the Bank of Israel and while the media gave the case close attention, the exposing newspaper came under severe criticism). Particular attention is given to the different way in which the newspaper (Haolam Hazeh) tried to deny the accusations of character assassination and the reasons why all its effects were to no avail.

KW: Corruption / Media / Politics / White collar crime

818 Harrison, J. 1983. "Crimes in High Places." *Israel Studies in Criminology* VI:105-30.

KW: White collar crime

819 Harrison, J. 1986. "White Collar and High Level Criminality: A Critical Appraisal of Criminology's Neglected Field." *Israel Studies in Criminology* VII:1-19.

KW: Criminological theories / White collar crime

820 Kwan, Q. Y., P. Rajeswaran, B. P. Parker and M. Amir. 1971. "The Role of Criminalistics in White-Collar Crimes." *Journal of Criminal Law, Criminology and Police Science* 62(3):437-49.

KW: Criminalistics / White collar crime

821 Mann, K. 1985. *Defending White-Collar Crime: A Portrait of Attorneys at Work.* New Haven, CT: Yale University Press.

KW: Attorneys / White collar crime

822 Mann, K., S. Wheeler and A. Sarat. 1980. "Sentencing the White-Collar Offender." *American Criminal Law Review* 17(4):479-500.

This is a field study of sentencing. The authors argue that while judges took a serious view of white-collar crime, they were often influenced by several factors to find a non-incarcerative disposition. Also, judges tended to rely predominantly on general deterrence as a rationale for sentencing in cases of white-collar crime.

KW: Courts / Sentencing / White collar crime

823 Sebba, L. 1985. "Attitudes of New Immigrants Toward White Collar Crime: A Cross-Cultural Exploration." *Human Relations* 36:1091-110. Also published as pp. 271-92 in *The Soviet Man in an Open Society*, edited by T. R. Horowitz. Lanham: University Press of America.

Examines the extent to which new immigrants from different societies and different economic climates (Soviet Union, United States) had different attitudes towards white collar crime. Russians were least critical of white collar crime, Israelis most and Americans in the middle.

KW: Attitudes / Comparative research / Cultural differences / Favoritism / New immigrants / Soviet Union / United States / White collar crime

824 Wheeler, S., K. Mann and A. Sarat. 1988. *Sitting in Judgement: The Sentencing of White-Collar Offenders*. New Haven, CT: Yale University Press.

KW: Courts / Offender / Sentencing / White collar crime

Author, Journal, and Subject Index

NOTE: Numbers following index entries correspond to page numbers in the book, not to reference number.

About the Compiler

ROBERT R. FRIEDMANN, Professor and Chair of the Department of Criminal Justice at Georgia State University in Atlanta, is also the founder and director of the Georgia criminal justice Statistical Analysis Bureau and of the Georgia-International Law Enforcement Exchange Program there. He has held teaching positions at the University of Haifa and the University of Minnesota. His research interests and published works focus on community policing. His most recent book is *Community Policing: Comparative Perspectives and Prospects* (1992), and he is currently editing a book on the state of criminal justice in Israel.

ISBN 0-313-29439-9

90000>

EAN

9 780313 294396

HARDCOVER BAR CODE